'This book is part exposé and part feminist manifesto. It builds on years of research and activism, and follows the invisible thread that connects the suicides of young women in remote corners of Italy to decisions made in corporate boardrooms, presidential palaces and the world's other corridors of power.

Following this thread has led me to painfully question my own online habits and my political stance on the digital revolution. Along the way, I've collected the stories of digital violence survivors and cyber psychologists, Congolese mothers and Chinese factory workers, algorithm designers and AI engineers, politicians and tech company delegates. I've also visited schools, universities, campaign organisations and houses of parliaments, and I've exposed myself to much more online misogynistic content I thought I had the stomach for.

From an investigation prompted by anger at specific cases, my quest turned into an arguably more complex project. What you are holding in your hand is an analysis of the tight relationship between three dominant forces of modern life: patriarchy, capitalism and technology – and a blueprint for positive change.'

DR LILIA GIUGNI

THE THRE@T

Why Digital Capitalism is Sexist
And How to Resist

THE THRE@T

LILIA GIUGNI

september

1 3 5 7 9 10 8 6 4 2

First published in 2022 by September Publishing

Typeset by RefineCatch Limited, www.refinecatch.com
Printed in Poland on paper from responsibly managed, sustainable sources by Hussar Books

ISBN 9781912836970
Ebook ISBN 9781912836987

September Publishing
www.septemberpublishing.org

To Carolina, Yu, Rose, Mirindi and Tiziana.
And to all the others, who mustn't be forgotten.

To my sisters (and siblings) in arms:
you know who you are.

And to my godmother Gigliola,
feminist ante-litteram, *who taught sex*
education in Catholic Southern Italy,
when sex was taboo and young women
were taught to behave themselves.
Who, more than anyone else,
encouraged me to believe in myself,
and to value a sharp mind
and a passionate heart.

I am no longer accepting the things I cannot change.
I am changing the things I cannot accept.
Attributed to Angela Y. Davis

Violence, in all its forms, is integral to the everyday functioning of capitalist society.
Cinzia Arruzza, Tithi Bhattacharya and Nancy Fraser

Technology is not neutral. We're inside of what
we make, and it's inside of us.
Donna J. Haraway

CONTENTS

Content warning

In this book you'll find a fair amount of sensitive content, including mentions of sexual assault, self-harm and suicide, and various forms of gender-based violence, abuse and exploitation.

INTRODUCTION

On the night between the 4th and 5th of January 2013, 14-year-old Carolina Picchio threw herself out of her bedroom window in Novara, Piedmont. She left a few messages: some for her loved ones, and some for the Internet users who had tormented her for weeks.

Two months before, Carolina had been to a party at a friend's house. They had ordered pizzas and passed round a few bottles of vodka, and Carolina had had a lot to drink. She was vomiting in the toilet and had almost passed out, when seven boys she was friendly with, more or less her age, came in and turned on their iPhone cameras. They cornered her, molested her and made sure to film every single moment. The morning after, they shared the videos on a school chat thread.

From private exchanges, the images quickly spread on social networks, where they attracted the attention of Carolina's friends and acquaintances, and of hundreds of strangers. Via Facebook and WhatsApp, she received over 2,600 insulting messages. She was called a 'slut' and was told she was 'disgusting' and that people would have liked to 'spit on her'. She had no memory of the night of the party, but was forced to re-experience it until she ceased to find her life worth living.

Despite several requests to do so, Mark Zuckerberg's platform, Facebook, did not remove the cyberbullies' comments until after Carolina's suicide.

* * *

On the 17th of March 2010, another teenager had jumped out of a window. Her name was Tian Yu, and the window was that of a Chinese factory where she worked over 12 hours per day assembling iPhones, such as those used by Carolina's persecutors.

That factory is part of a humongous complex owned by Foxconn, a multinational electronics supplier to which Apple and other tech giants outsource the manufacturing of their appliances. Yu's family, living in the countryside, struggled to make ends meet, so she had become a factory worker to help them pay their bills. When she signed her first contract with Foxconn, Yu was about three years older than Carolina.

Every morning, Yu woke up at 6.30 a.m., attended a compulsory unpaid meeting at 7.20 a.m. and did not leave her position in the assembly line until 7.40 p.m., usually being forced to skip dinner to work overtime. She had to ask permission to use the toilet and the walls around her were covered in posters with 'motivational' sentences such as 'Growth, thy name is suffering' and 'A harsh environment is a good thing'.

When Yu jumped out of the building, Foxconn owed her a month's salary plus overtime pay because of an administrative oversight. She had no money left and her mobile phone had broken, leaving her unable to ask for help. Neither could she reach out to any of her co-workers; they were all so exhausted that they had never talked to one another before.

You will be glad to know that, unlike Carolina Picchio, Tian Yu survived her fall. She remained, however, paralysed from the waist down. In 2010 alone, 17 other workers from the same Foxconn factory attempted suicide, and most of them succeeded. Apple founder Steve Jobs defended his subcontractor, arguing that suicides at Foxconn were 'below China's national average'.

* * *

This book looks at what is perhaps the most important event of the last 30 years: the *digital revolution*. It looks at it through the eyes of the women who are harmed by it globally. These women come from all walks of life. Some of them, like Carolina Picchio, are victimised through digital devices. Others, like Tian Yu, are exploited while producing them. And some do not even have access to the Internet, but are brutally raped in wars funded by minerals that make our tablets work.

After years of unimpeded enthusiasm towards all things tech, our views have become more critical and nuanced. For example, we have started to pay attention to controversial practices such as data mining, online surveillance and algorithmic bias. We are also increasingly aware of the relationship between technology and gender inequalities (among other things, we speak a lot of 'online hate' against women and LGBTQ+ people). But we have only just started to connect the dots, and the more connections we draw, the less pleasant the picture is to look at. As I write, millions of women across the world are violated, exploited and marginalised due to processes of technological change, and in many more ways than we may realise.

I will attempt to shed light on how all this might have happened, proposing an explanation based on the tight intersections between technology, patriarchy and capitalism. Because the heart of the matter, in my opinion, is precisely that the digital revolution has taken place in a capitalistic and patriarchal society. This has profoundly shaped the way digital devices are designed and built, how we utilise them and who does or does not have access to them, which can cause considerable repercussions for women's civil and social rights.

Just to clarify, I *won't* be trying to convince you that the advent of digital technologies has had no benefits for women, or for the rest of humankind. Like all of you, I am grateful for the tools that allow me to access information, connect with my friends and family, and simplify my daily tasks. After all, I am writing on a laptop with a Wi-Fi connection, making massive use of online archives and search engines. As a feminist, I also appreciate the role that digital innovations have played in campaigns such as #MeToo and #InternationalWomensStrike, and in helping entire generations of women (including my own) organise and support one another. Of this, however, we know much already. I believe it is the dark side of digital capitalism that should once and for all come to light, together with the strategies to resist.

It also seems to me that we should look at the problem systemically, rather than simply focusing on the aspects that feel closest to home, or in which we can recognise ourselves. I must confess that when I started researching this book I, too, had mostly in mind stories that resonated with me on a personal level, like that of Carolina

Picchio: a girl who came from the same country as me, and whom it was natural for me to picture as a little sister, or a younger version of myself. But one story leads to another, and the more I explored the ecosystem where tragedies such as Carolina's developed, the more I encountered experiences like Tian Yu's. In the end, I was convinced that it was urgent and necessary to try to explain the links between these different stories, which are equally unacceptable and underpinned by the same power relations.

And now just a couple of necessary clarifications. When I say that I'd like to offer a *global* and *systemic* examination of the digital revolution and of its gendered effects, I do not mean that my own perspective is all-encompassing or universal. Any viewpoint on a given subject is unavoidably influenced by the position from which we observe it. And, of course, it is from a specific point within the *global system* that I am writing these pages and that you are reading them. Plus, my evaluations are also filtered through my own personal circumstances: those of a Southern Italian woman who makes a living as a university researcher in the UK, who can access information in some languages but not others, and who has experienced several of the forms of violence and marginalisation described in this book, but most certainly not all of them. (I, too, for instance, have suffered online harassment, but I've never worked in a factory.) So, in my writing I have done my very best to distinguish my reflections from the accounts I have collected, which I believe can speak for themselves.

Finally, I want to make it plain that I do not consider gender the only relevant lens through which to examine what is happening to us. It is, clearly, not only women who pay a price for the latest technological changes, and some women undoubtedly have it tougher than others. I have strived as much as possible to adopt in my analysis an intersectional approach: i.e. one sensitive to how women's lives are influenced by factors such as their class, race, sexuality, physical ability and geography.

At the same time, like many feminists before me, I am also convinced that we should reclaim the notion of *woman* as a political category and put it at the centre of both our examination of social phenomena and our fights for a freer, more equal and fairer world. Let's put it like that. Still today, our societies treat women as *the other* – a subaltern subject whose voice and needs are ignored every time we try to develop an accurate view of what's going on in the world. And the digital revolution is certainly no exception. This is why, if we want to judge it more honestly, I think it is from women's voices and women's needs that we should start, however heterogenous they may be.

Not to mention that *placing women at the centre* is helpful not only when diagnosing a social problem, but also when searching for solutions. This is something I'll talk about in Part 3 of the book, where you'll find a few ideas and proposals aimed at *taking back the tech*: that is to say, turning technology into a truly emancipatory force and a leverage to create a better and more just future for women and for all. These inputs are grounded in my years of research and activism at the intersection between digital rights and social and gender justice. But you should know that, most of all, they are inspired by the testimonies of the women you'll read about. My primary goal is to do them justice, and I am certain that, much more than me, they will persuade you that the time has come to face reality and start fighting for better technology and a better world.

AUTHOR'S NOTE

In this book I will talk a lot about the interconnections between *patriarchy*, *capitalism* and *technology*. A great deal has been written on each of these three concepts (some of which you will find in the References at the back of this book, all searchable through relevant phrases, together with the various sources I used). But before you read any further, you may like to know more about what I, personally, mean by these three terms.

Both patriarchy and capitalism are, in my mind, two *dominant logics* within our societies – in other words, two enormously influential systems of beliefs and practices, which determine how we all organise our lives and daily activities. While very different, I also find that patriarchy and capitalism have several things in common.

First of all, they are both extremely resilient, for a number of reasons. When a way of organising society survives for several centuries (in the case of patriarchy, even for millenniums), it is normally because somebody profits from it. Indeed, both patriarchy and capitalism allocate power and resources based, respectively, on gender and class (as well as on geographical and racial differences). To put it another way: they both have their winners and losers, and it is not in the winners' interest to change the rules of the game.

7

Another characteristic that capitalism and patriarchy share is their extraordinary capacity to adapt, which has allowed them to take different forms throughout history. There are important differences between, say, the industrial capitalism of the eighteenth–nineteenth centuries and our current digital capitalism, or between the US and Chinese economies. The same applies to patriarchy: gender relations changed notably over the last few centuries, but still today it feels quite different to grow up as a girl (or a boy, or a queer person) in Sweden or Saudi Arabia. On the whole, however, many foundational elements of the two logics remain the same. In all its various incarnations, capitalism still relies on, among other things, waged labour and the appropriation and accumulation of resources. Likewise, patriarchy continues, to this day, to establish gender hierarchies that might have become more subtle, but are by no means less powerful.

Several authors before me have taken an interest in how capitalism and patriarchy influence each other, and I'll examine some of their ideas. The uniqueness of this book, though, lies in its exploring how capitalism and patriarchy interact with yet another force – technology – and more specifically with the digital tools that have recently revolutionised our existence: think smartphones, social media, search algorithms, data-mining techniques.

Some may find it odd to see things we use daily associated with abstract and grand concepts such as patriarchy and capitalism. But, as we shall see, many of the technologies we know and love, just like their processes of production and distribution, are rife with capitalistic and patriarchal injustices.

PART 1

Digital revolution and vicious circles

CHAPTER 1

Patriarchy 4.0

Not that long ago, British Labour MP Jess Phillips accompanied her 11-year-old son to get a book signed by his favourite author. She noticed that the boy, initially very excited, had begun to look anxious, and kept his back glued to the wall. She wondered whether he might be intimidated by the prospect of meeting his hero, but her son told her, 'It's very crowded in there, Mum. It's best if we stay here, where I don't risk being attacked.'

While trying to reassure her child, Jess cannot afford the luxury of considering his worries excessive, or letting him live a normal childhood. The police visit their home regularly and have encouraged her to have a panic room fitted in her office, and a locksmith has strengthened the security in her Birmingham house. Before running for election, Jess worked at a women's aid charity and once elected she brought her feminist views into Parliament. Since she was first elected in 2015, she has criticised gender inequalities within her own party's executive bodies as vehemently as the anti-domestic-violence policies of the Tory government. These stances have gained her many enemies, who use social media to make her life impossible.

Everything started in 2015, when Jess had a squabble with a Conservative politician, Philip Davies. During a backbench committee meeting, he suggested that the House of Commons host an event to commemorate International Men's Day. As the only woman on the committee, Jess replied that, to her, every day felt like International Men's Day. Within a few hours, her newsfeed and message boxes filled up with chilling messages. Internet users wrote that she deserved to see her sons hanged on a tree, that they wanted to murder her and lock her in a basement to 'pour molten iron' into her vagina 'until she started vomiting' and 'repeatedly rape her to watch her spirit die'.

Since then, the online assaults have repeated themselves as regular as clockwork, especially on Facebook, Twitter and YouTube. Once, Jess received over 600 social media threats in a single night. Nor had her tormentors had enough: the day after, she was forced to put up with a new wave of comments, which, this time, declared her 'too ugly to rape'. She dutifully reported the abuse to the relevant social network companies, but mostly to no avail.

Over time, the Birmingham Yardley MP started to suffer from anxiety and panic attacks. While determined not to let herself be affected by the aggressions, she cannot help but think of her colleague and close friend Jo Cox, who was stabbed on the street by a right-wing extremist after having been regularly victimised on the Web. And it doesn't take a genius to understand that the longer threats against female politicians circulate online, the more likely it is that someone may turn them into actions. Suffice it to say that a man has already been arrested for hiding outside Jess's constituency office with the intention of attacking her.

To this day, Jess Phillips continues to fight for legal interventions aiming to make digital companies more accountable on matters of online violence. When, a couple of years ago, I met her in her Westminster office, she talked to me at length of the three things she found most difficult to bear.

The first was having to invest in her protection the time and energy she would have otherwise devoted to her work and her loved ones. The second was the impact of the abuse on her family, and on the numerous young women who follow her parliamentary activities, many of whom are appalled by the way she is treated and are now afraid of going into politics or even speaking up on the Internet. And the third thing was social media firms' reluctance, in spite of their powerful means and fat profits, to stop the war on women that has been declared on their platforms.

* * *

Let's play a simple game. You tell me what social networks you use (or, if you don't use any, which ones you have seen being used by your best friend, daughter, neighbour, etc.) and I'll tell you how women and girls are treated in those spaces.

Let's start with Facebook, the biggest social media platform on the planet, counting (at the time of writing) about 42 million users in the UK and almost 3 billion globally. Women's and men's experiences of the site, as revealed by several studies, differ rather significantly. The NGO Plan International, for example, has recently surveyed over 14,000 young women worldwide, and discovered that almost

40 per cent of them had been threatened or attacked on Facebook. The second alarming finding: Black, Brown and queer girls are even more at risk, since they attract abuse motivated by both their gender and their racial, sexual or cultural identities. And increasingly robust scientific literature helps us identify other particularly exposed groups: disabled young women[1] and Jewish and Muslim women, regardless of their age.

After Facebook, the worst platforms on which to be a woman seem to be Instagram and WhatsApp, both owned by the same corporate group founded by Mark Zuckerberg, which in 2021 changed its name from Facebook to Meta. Instagram and WhatsApp, just like Facebook itself, are plagued by non-consensual pornography – an exceptionally gruesome form of digital violence, which I will discuss in detail later. To get a sense of the scale of the problem, you only need to look at users' removal requests. According to several journalistic sources, Meta processes about 500,000 of them every month, all concerning intimate videos or pictures shared without the permission of the people (mostly, the women) appearing in them.

Things are no better on Twitter, a smaller platform but commonly used to comment on politics and current affairs, particularly in English-speaking countries. This characteristic makes it a very toxic arena for politically active women: not only lawmakers like Jess Phillips (or, on the other side of the Atlantic, Alexandria Ocasio-Cortez and Kamala Harris), but also writers, journalists

---

1   Some people and communities prefer the expression 'disabled woman' (or man, or person), while others deem the term 'woman with disability' more appropriate. Even within disability justice movements, the question as to which term to use remains open. This is why throughout this book I have decided to use both definitions interchangeably.

and campaigners. In 2018, Amnesty International monitored the tweets addressed to some of these women during 'hot periods', such as election campaigns, and calculated they had received a message classified as 'violent' or 'hostile' every 30 seconds on average (victimisation rates were, once again, especially high among Black and Muslim women).

Video-sharing platforms like YouTube and TikTok have their own unique pitfalls. They host staggering volumes of non-consensual pornography and abusive messages directed towards female users and are used for sharing misogynistic ideas and hate speech based on gender, race, religion and sexuality. YouTube, in particular, is swamped with videos teaching how to 'burst the lies women tell on rape', or vilifying and sometimes explicitly threatening female celebrities and politicians. It was on YouTube, as it happens, that Jess Phillips got targeted for several years by a number of sexist vloggers. One of them, UKIP's former candidate to the European Parliament Carl Benjamin, abused her for months before the platform finally prevented him from monetising his uploads.

Now, let me deal with objections on the lines of *But feminists like Jess Phillips were a target well before the advent of social media.* This is certainly true and I would be the last person to deny that our political history is filled with attempts to clip women's wings and undermine their struggles. I happen to have a passion for biographies of women activists from past centuries and the similarities between the present day and, say, the intimidation campaigns orchestrated against early-twentieth-century suffragettes are not lost on me. Even the special ferocity reserved for minority women is, unfortunately, hardly new. Let us remember that Simone Veil, a Jew, an Auschwitz survivor and the main sponsor of France's abortion legislation in the 1970s, had swastikas drawn on her car and received a deluge of anonymous letters stating that 'the true holocaust was that of unborn children'.

If only for the sake of intellectual and political honesty, though, we should acknowledge that the digital revolution has opened novel and unsettling scenarios. To begin with, it has made public figures like Jess Phillips (or, say, Cambridge classicist Mary Beard, British Labour MP Diane Abbott, or feminist advocate Caroline Criado Perez) even more vulnerable than they previously were. And this is not just about new vehicles for threats and harassment. Many other aspects make digital attacks unique, the first of which is their intrusiveness and their capacity to reach a woman wherever she is, at any time of the day. 'I get those comments when I least expect them: as I walk down the street, or when I am at home on the sofa with my husband or my kids,' Jess Phillips explained to me during our chat at Westminster. 'You can choose not to open an anonymous letter, or to only read correspondence in the office. But you cannot always keep your phone turned off. And, in my case, managing my social media accounts is part of my MP job. I cannot get rid of them, and I wouldn't think it fair to entirely delegate this to my staff.'

On the flip side, we should bear in mind that public-facing women like Jess tend at least to have access to resources and support. Yet millions of Internet users around the world cannot count on any special protections and they have also become easy prey. Just consider a couple of stats. According to recent estimates, over one third of women globally have experienced some form of digital violence. And if we move from the figures capturing the scale of the phenomenon to those documenting its long-term consequences, the picture gets bleaker and bleaker. You may want to look, for instance, at a recently published inquiry commissioned by *The Economist* (see

References). The research team found that 35 per cent of online abuse victims surveyed internationally had experienced mental health problems, with almost three quarters of them, at some point, worrying about their physical safety. Fear of new aggressions – the study also shows – pushed nine surveyed women out of ten to modify their digital habits and 7 per cent of them to change their job.

Should you need more names and more life stories to bring this data to life, I have more examples. There is British Channel 4 journalist and news presenter Cathy Newman, a regular target of Internet vitriol, who told me the price she pays for the unapologetically feminist stances she takes online is being constantly on guard. 'I built a career in a male-dominated industry, which has made me resilient. But when digital onslaughts come in waves it is actually scary,' she said to me when we chatted about her experiences of various social media platforms. Among other instances, Cathy spoke to me of when the attacks peaked following an interview she had done with controversial Canadian academic Jordan Peterson. Channel 4 was forced to call in security experts and more than once she had people shouting at her on the street.

And there is more. There's the story of British Labour politician Jessica Asato, who in 2015 ran as parliamentary candidate for Norwich North. She told me one of the reasons she had no intention of running again was the barrage of verbal abuse she had to bear during the election campaign.

There's a Cambridge colleague of mine (who wished to remain anonymous), who found out to her dismay that her feminist publications have made her end up in the Internet trolls' black book. She is now extremely careful not to share anything online that could direct them towards her kids: no holiday pictures, no posts that many a mum beaming with pride would write after their child's school play. She is too frightened that among all those who write to her 'Watch yourself' and 'Watch your family', at least a couple may actually mean it.

Then there are the testimonies of the young girls I meet in schools, who cannot even imagine a life without social networks. But when I ask them how old they were when they were first harassed on Instagram or TikTok, they overwhelmingly answer: 'Umm, perhaps I was 11.' And so on and so forth, girl after girl, woman after woman.

Yet the thing is, you are holding this book in your hands. That makes me think that you don't need any further anecdotes to be persuaded of the gravity of the situation, or of the fact that we all stand to lose if online violence turns into a means to silence women and sabotage their careers and lives. I suppose, instead, that you are grappling with a number of questions on what's behind all this. Perhaps you have one main question: *What on earth are digital platforms doing to tackle this tsunami of misogynistic abuse?*

The (not-so-reassuring) answer is below.

* * *

To be entirely fair, I do have at least one reassuring piece of news and that is that many women have no intention of letting themselves be sabotaged and silenced. From the struggles of well-known targets of online harassment to the work of grassroots organisations speaking up for less visible and less wealthy survivors, over the last few years a formidable resistance movement has emerged. Women from all countries and all backgrounds have organised to lobby social media companies and have attracted a great deal of media attention, securing support from prestigious human rights organisations, as well as from United Nations agencies and sectors of the European Commission.

This is why, predictably enough, social media companies have decided to batten down the hatches. Facebook/Meta, Twitter, YouTube and TikTok have all adopted ad hoc internal guidelines through which they prohibit threats, harassment and hate speech on their platforms. They have also ratified the EU Code of Conduct on countering illegal hate speech: an initiative that binds them to more effectively remove content undermining the dignity of several at-risk categories; a step advertised with great pomp by their press offices.

But I'm afraid that despite all the promising and the debating, Big Tech's response to the sacrosanct requests of women who expect to feel safe on the Internet has largely stayed the same and this throws under the bus yet another group of women who are invisible on the other side of the screen.

I'd like you to meet one of them, a social media content moderator named Isabella Plunkett. Isabella is about 27 years old and works for Covalen, one of the many contractors to which Facebook/Meta delegates the task of 'cleaning up' its sites and apps. She has much to say about the only actual operational solution platforms have so far adopted against digital violence: the ex-post moderation of what is published online.

Let me explain this as plainly as possible. In practice, every time an abusive comment, like those directed towards Jess Phillips, is uploaded, it is a person like Isabella Plunkett who reviews it and who, potentially, deletes it. To this day, only a part of these operations can be entrusted to automatic moderation software, which is still unable to grasp with sufficient accuracy the complex decisions required in the evaluation of, at times, very sophisticated text and images. Precisely because human intervention continues to be necessary (and, according to experts, it will long remain so), all the main social media platforms have created positions like Isabella Plunkett's.

During her workday, Isabella looks at about 100 tickets (meaning posts including videos, pictures or text) and has a handful of minutes to decide whether to eliminate them or leave them online. On a daily basis, she skims through a wide range of triggering materials: from paedo-pornographic images, to clips of killings and suicides. As a result of staring at all sorts of horrors she started to have nightmares and needed to take antidepressants. In case you were wondering, we know of Isabella's situation because in spring 2021 she chose to testify to an Irish parliamentary committee on the treatment of online moderators, revealing her name and identity. It was a courageous decision, considering that when hired she had to sign a non-disclosure agreement (NDA), exposing her to legal retribution if she divulged details of her job, even to family and friends.

'I usually do battle with these things myself; I am the sort of person who feels like they can take on all challenges. But when you're in that position and especially when you sign an NDA saying you can't speak to your friends and family about these things and you're not receiving the appropriate support in work, what are you supposed to do? Are you supposed to sit in the dark? Are you supposed to be alone on these matters?' Isabella said later.

Isabella explained to Irish parliamentarians that she was denied permission to work from home during the Covid-19 pandemic, despite having vulnerable relatives shielding at home. A minority of her colleagues, who were directly employed by Meta, seemed to have had the opportunity to work remotely, something that increased Isabella's workload, since the most explicit and violent content, usually marked as priority, can only be moderated from office computers.

Another relevant fact to understand Isabella's difficulties is that during the last six years Meta has notably expanded its moderation programme, creating a total of 15,000 new jobs. However, the corporation decided to economise, keeping just a small amount of the moderation work in-house and subcontracting much of it to intermediary companies. To quantify the value of this financial speculation, we only need a couple of rapid calculations. According to a recent appraisal, the median Meta employee earns about $240,000 annually in salary, bonuses and stock options. Content moderators working for third parties, on the contrary, may earn about $29,000 dollars, significantly less if hired in other continents (say, in Latvia, Kenya, India or the Philippines, where several subcontractors have relocated their activities). I'll let you make of this information what you will.

'The pay of Facebook staff is more than double mine,' specified Isabella. 'If our work is so important, why are we not Facebook staff? [...] content moderation is Facebook's core business [...] We should not be treated as disposable.' She added that she and her co-workers were 'tired of the second-class citizenship' and that she hoped the committee would 'investigate this practice of outsourcing'.

Meta is in no way the only company to have made the choice to outsource moderation work. Twitter and YouTube, for their part, have long adopted identical tactics. For a while now, both of them have relied on a workforce located in Manila, where, reportedly, staffers may have to review up to 1,000 contents per day, often in foreign languages, and are subject to restricted toilet breaks. In an attempt to draw foreign investment, Filipino labour laws grant very limited protections to local workers, which in turn enables international corporations to save a great deal of money.

This is, incidentally, one of the reasons why Isabella Plunkett decided to testify publicly. She was aware of the risks she exposed herself to, but she felt she ought to speak up not only for herself, but also on behalf of her co-workers in non-Western countries, who are even more vulnerable than she is. 'I speak out today to make a difference,' she declared very openly. 'The mental health aspect [...] The content that is moderated is awful. It would affect anyone. It has finally started to get to me.' As we shall see, it has started to get to many of her fellow moderators worldwide.

* * *

A couple of years ago a social media page of mine was vandalised with violent pornographic material, which seemed to include young teenagers – children. Due to my line of work, I am rather well prepared for these occurrences (and I know only too well that some women have it even tougher). So I diligently reviewed the safety options of my profile, flagged the posts to the platform and contacted the IT offices of the university where I work and the organisations with which I collaborate to warn them in case the attack was redirected from my page to their own. Then, all of a sudden, an image got stuck in my head. I pictured the woman who, in that exact moment, was processing my notification and presumably had to go through those images before eliminating them. I felt livid with anger, thinking that we were both trapped: the moderator at her workstation, crunching one ticket after another, and I, undoubtedly more privileged, yet still at the mercy of the misogynistic culture infesting the Web. It is hardly a coincidence that imagining a woman beyond the screen has come so naturally to me.

In truth, there is barely any data disaggregated by gender on the global online moderation workforce. Silicon Valley giants and their intermediaries tend to be very reticent on the specifics of their operations and it is only very recently that a few journalistic inquiries, field studies and revelations of whistle-blowers, like Isabella Plunkett, have begun to throw light on the matter. Still, there are many indications that women moderators face additional hurdles, gender-specific ones.

To start with, the fact that much Internet violence is motivated by gender seems to intensify the emotional weight of the job for female employees. Not for nothing, the first lawsuit for mental health damages ever filed against Facebook was initiated by two women. One of them, American moderator Erin Elder, suffered serious trauma after she had to watch, again and again, a video showing a teen girl being gang-raped by men on a lawn. She asked her manager if she could access any psychological support and was told that her direct employer, a firm called PRO Unlimited, did not offer more than a counselling session every four months, while Facebook did not regard improving that service as part of its remit. Erin's co-plaintiff, Selena Scola, said that she witnessed thousands of acts of extreme and graphic violence 'from her cubicle in Facebook's Silicon Valley offices' and that she developed PTSD 'as a result of constant and unmitigated exposure'.

It is, in fact, a cruel paradox that the women burdened with the task of cleaning up social media develop the very same pathologies afflicting survivors of online violence. And, sadly, their mental health appears to be anything but a priority for their employers.

Another US moderator named Chloe (pseudonym) revealed to *The Verge* magazine that even during the training phase at the beginning of her employment contract she had started to show the symptoms experienced by many of her colleagues: a sense of impending terror, sudden bursts of sobbing, suffocating anxiety. Her line manager, though, had simply advised her to focus on her breath and not to let herself be too affected by what she watched. According to Chloe, while being kind enough to her, the man had one main objective in mind: he wanted his subordinates to feel well enough to carry on working as 'Internet cleaners'.

Perhaps unsurprisingly, given their extremely oppressive working conditions, non-Western women moderators face even stronger repercussions. Just like Isabella Plunkett, many of them are forced to sign harsh confidentiality agreements and they generally speak to journalists or researchers only upon conditions of anonymity. Yet, when they do, their accounts are among the most disturbing of all.

Take that of Maria (pseudonym), a Filipino young woman who dreamed of studying medicine, who was also bound by an NDA. She could still describe in detail a video she had had to stomach years before and which had never stopped haunting her. 'There's this lady. Probably in the age of 15 to 18, I don't know. She looks like a minor. There's this bald guy putting his head to the lady's vagina. The lady is blindfolded, handcuffed, screaming, and crying.' The video was more than 30 minutes long, but Maria started shaking with rage and revulsion after just over a minute. 'I don't know if I can forget it. I watched that a long time ago, but it's like I just watched it yesterday.'

Among the testimonies of other Filipino moderators, there are those of several working mothers who had been forced to watch so many videos of bestiality with children that they would no longer leave their kids alone with babysitters. There are, tragically, cases of suicides within the workforce.

Regardless of their geographical location, we need to account for the dehumanising atmosphere that is said to characterise many moderation offices, which seems to affect female employees more deeply than anyone else. For example, several women employed by specialised moderation contractor Cognizant told the press they had found pubic hair on their desks. Others were sexually harassed by male colleagues, perhaps aroused by the extreme pornography passing by every day on their screens. And so it goes on, a catalogue of endless miseries.

That being said, what should fill us with inspiration is how moderators have so far organised to resist, with their initiatives recently beginning to bear fruit. A number of digital platforms have lately compensated former moderators for health damages and are partnering with their contractors to offer the workforce extra emotional support. Yet the measures introduced so far are still fundamentally inadequate and Isabella Plunkett's story is once again a case in point.

When Isabella's evidence caused a stir internationally, her employer declared that they had introduced '24/7 health support and wellness coaching on site' and that 'this team provides 1:1 counselling support for all employees'.

The downside to this is that the 'wellness teams' did not involve psychologists or psychiatrists, whom people like Isabella would need to consult about the mental health issues they have developed on the job. The 'coaches' Isabella has access to are, instead, much cheaper for the firm and, in her own words, 'mean really well but they are not doctors.' They might, for one thing, advise her that spending some time painting or doing karaoke could help her feel a bit better. Yet 'one does not always feel like singing' declared Isabella half sarcastically, half exasperatedly. Especially 'after having seen someone be battered to bits.'

* * *

The lives of women like Jess Phillips and Isabella Plunkett might seem worlds apart, but they are two sides of the same coin: unspeakable online misogyny and the (exploitative) work necessary to cover it up.

Seen together, in my opinion, these stories tell us at least two important things. First, that the digital revolution has paved the way for new, gendered forms of abuse. And second, that when women start protesting, social media companies tend to react by slapping a Band-Aid on whatever aspect of the problem we have all begun to worry about. Never mind if that causes further suffering. It so happens that billion-dollar corporations respond to the demands of women like Jess Phillips, who want to see their rights protected online, by violating the rights of other women, like Isabella Plunkett.

As you may perhaps imagine, some commentators suggest that we cannot have our cake and eat it: to put it bluntly, we must choose between safeguarding the Jesses or the Isabellas of this world. Am I the only one who finds this idea not only ridiculous, but also morally repellent? Not to mention that narratives like *You ladies wanted online safety? Now shut up and deal with moderators getting PTSD* appear in all their dishonesty when we consider that it's the very business model of many social media platforms that favour violent online practices (a crucial matter that I will return to).

But there is also a larger point to be made. In my mind, it should come as no surprise that modern digital capitalism compromises the well-being of women, and that it sometimes does so in the name of other women's protection. Far from being a novelty, this dynamic is typical of all previous incarnations of the capitalist logic, intersected as this was, from day one, with the logic of patriarchy.

Here's an obvious yet highly significant example. For centuries, the global economy has relied on the unpaid care labour of women birthing and raising the future workforce. When, throughout history, women strived for economic independence and for gender parity across all professions, fully satisfying their requests would have required a complete overthrow of the economic foundations of society. Among other changes, care activities would have had to be more fairly distributed between genders, and, very possibly, everybody's working hours would have needed reducing, while welfare provisions for families would have needed extending. In fact, the reverse happened. To survive and to keep making money, the system created new and insidious traps for all categories of women and generated further hierarchies to divide them. Newly emancipated female professionals were asked to work extra hours, in the home and outside it. Meanwhile, a part of their care labour was reallocated to less privileged women, often from a migrant and non-white background (think of the many cleaners and carers who have come to populate our cities since more Western, middle-class women have joined the labour market). Divide and conquer is, after all, one of the best proven strategies of all time.

Very clearly, a similar mechanism is at work today, within an economy redesigned by digital technologies. And the bitter truth is that this vicious circle seems to repeat itself indefinitely. As I write, online abuse survivors like Jess Phillips fight for more stringent regulation of social media platforms. Moderators like Isabella Plunkett – most of them in Western countries, where stronger unions and labour legislation give them more room for manoeuvre – try to force the very same businesses to grant them decent working conditions. Both campaigns deserve our full attention and our staunch support, and both groups are snatching important victories. But there is a risk that the companies may react as they have always done so far: by attending to the most pressing reputational damages, to the detriment of other women with less opportunity to stand up for themselves.

Just to cite one of the most blatant cases: Facebook/Meta has recently invested more than any other tech company in the prevention of online violence in Europe and in English-speaking countries. Allegedly, however, it did not see fit to do the same in the Global South, where it was under less pressure from media, governments and society. Even the compensation the corporation has granted to content moderators suffering health damages has so far predominantly been in the Western labour force. And, in the face of ongoing labour disputes, a likely outcome is the relocation of an even larger proportion of moderation activities to continents with less rigorous labour laws.

So it is up to us to keep our eyes and ears wide open. To support, with no exclusion, the claims of women who have been harmed by the worst sides of digital capitalism and to avoid being deceived by narratives that present the oppression of some of us as a necessary and unavoidable evil.

CHAPTER 2

Algorithmic injustices

In 2018, Janey Webb made a living as an Uber driver in Iowa, in the Midwestern United States. She was eagerly awaiting the weekend of the 4th of July, when millions of Americans celebrate Independence Day, many of them travelling using apps like Uber and Lyft. That weekend, though, Janey did not cash in a single cent. A few days earlier, her account had been blocked by Uber, which in several countries uses a facial-recognition software to verify the identity of its drivers.

Janey Webb is a trans woman and as she has undergone her gender transition process her appearance has changed. She tried multiple times to upload more recent pictures of her face, but having registered some differences between these photos and the one on her driving licence, Uber's software suspended her profile and denied her the opportunity to work.

Uber is one of the most controversial tech firms in the world and I'll return shortly to its worst internal practices. For context, however, you should know that in 2018 the company received no fewer than 3,045 sexual assault reports from US female passengers molested by their male drivers and from female drivers assaulted by their male customers. It was precisely to respond to related accusations of negligence that the company launched the new identification technology used by Janey Webb. Except the system, the introduction of which had been advertised as a 'great investment in the safety and well-being of both passengers and drivers' and even as 'an act of care' and a tool 'respectful of everyone's privacy', was simply unable to acknowledge that among Uber drivers there could be a transgender woman.

'A trans person can't be expected to update their license every three months or so just to avoid being deactivated,' said Janey exasperatedly, after having driven for two hours to sort out the incident at Uber's only in-person support centre in her home state. It is helpful to remind ourselves that trans women like Janey often face great difficulties in finding stable and decently paid jobs. This is why – exactly like women of colour and other traditionally marginalised groups – they frequently work in precarious conditions within the gig economy (the sector where, instead of a regular wage, you get paid for the gigs you do, offering services through platforms such as Uber). The fact that Uber's labour force is made up of gig workers rather than employees with historically recognised rights plays an important part in Janey's story.

After a few days, Janey managed to get her account reactivated. However, neither her expenses nor her lost fares were refunded by the platform and she was told that the company's management had no intention of amending the software to avoid future problems. Meanwhile, other trans women began to speak publicly of their experiences with the same technology, complaining that they had missed a huge number of the fares on which they relied to pay their bills. Several UK-based Black drivers also had their accounts frozen and began to suspect that the technology worked less effectively with non-white people. In all of these cases, Uber attempted to gloss over the incidents and refused to acknowledge the workers' claims.

Whatever Uber might wish us to believe, there is conclusive evidence of the discriminating effects of facial-recognition technology. Recent research has confirmed, for instance, that this technology makes regular mistakes when analysing Black women (whom they mistake for men), as well as trans and non-binary people (whom they associate to the wrong gender or even completely fail to detect). In other words, even if a trans person like Janey Webb did her best to continuously update her ID, there is a concrete risk that the system might be unable to process her images correctly. Neither are discriminations based on gender, race and sexual identities the only distortions we should be wary of: several disabled activists have already warned that facial-recognition technology struggles to recognise people with craniofacial disorders and other conditions that alter the face.

The consequences of this go well beyond lost earnings within the gig economy. Among other things, facial-identification AI is now used for purposes as varied as registering on dating apps, at the airport and during policing and law enforcement procedures. Just try to imagine how you'd feel if you were stopped just as you were getting on a plane and were forced to go through mortifying personal questioning in order to prove you are what you say on your passport.

Do you think that sounds very much like a dystopian novel? Just read on.

* * *

On the Internet, misogyny, racism, homophobia, transphobia and many other forms of prejudice and abuse do not only manifest themselves as social media harassment. The digital revolution has also triggered different, subtler types of injustice, embedded in the very functioning of cutting-edge technology.

'You have training sets that are used to teach a computer to see a face. So you have lots of examples of faces. But if the faces you're providing aren't that diverse, then the system you end up creating might have a harder time detecting people who aren't represented in the set,' explains Joy Buolamwini with clarity. She is a Ghanaian-American-Canadian, a computer scientist and 'poet of code' at MIT's Media Lab in Cambridge, Massachusetts and the author of one of the research studies mentioned above. Consider that Joy knows a thing or two about algorithmic oppression, having developed an interest in this area after experimenting herself with a facial-detection tool for a university project and discovering that it did not recognise her Black woman's face.

Let me be very clear on one point. Facial-recognition technology is very contentious even beyond its tendency to misclassify specific social groups. It is, in truth, the very existence of tools able to detect someone's gender or other personal characteristics starting from an image that opens a black hole of unsettling possibilities. If these technologies ended up, say, in the hands of the many governments that still criminalise alternative gender and sexual identities, oppress ethnic minorities or restrict women's freedom of movement, they could easily be turned into instruments of surveillance and persecution.

That being said, Joy's explanation fits, with minimal variations, to a wide range of AI technologies. Lots of them are rather different from facial analysis, but they all have one thing in common: while being, in theory, extremely advanced and 'objective' tools, they contribute to the ongoing marginalisation of women and other historically subaltern groups. Indeed, many AI systems are programmed based on large samples of pre-existing data. Numerous datasets, however, already contain distortions reflecting the invisibility queer women like Janey Webb or women of colour like Joy Buolamwini have long faced in our societies. As a consequence, algorithms of all sorts will learn through time to reproduce those biases and exacerbate existing disparities.

So, since examples of algorithmic discrimination are as numerous as they are troubling, I have got for you a list of the most recent and the most striking.

In 2019, an African American woman named Crystal Marie McDaniels was denied the mortgage she and her husband (who is also Black) needed to buy a house. They had already paid thousands of dollars in administrative fees and both had a job, savings and a good credit history. Yet Crystal Marie was told that since the company she worked for as a marketer had taken her on as a contractor, the lending agency did not see her application as sufficiently strong. As it happens, however, several white colleagues of hers, also hired as contractors, had been granted mortgages in the past. There's an important detail to be noted: the decision to reject Crystal Marie's application was influenced by one of the many algorithmic programs that lenders use to filter their applicants. 'I think it would be really naive for someone like myself to not consider that race played a role in the process,' said Crystal Marie to non-profit news agency The Markup. Coincidentally, that very same year The Markup launched a study on disparities in credit allocations in the USA. It found that even when candidates of colour had solid financial positions, they were still significantly less likely than white applicants to obtain a positive response. According to The Markup, lenders' algorithms played an important part in fostering distortions based on both gender and race.

Paradigmatic case number two. In 2018, Amazon was forced to withdraw an AI recruiting tool on which the company's own developers had worked for a very long time, which helped select job candidates' CVs and cover letters. Trained on a historical archive of job applications received by the firm (which, as we shall see, has a long history of internal gender and racial inequalities), the system had 'taught itself' to prefer male applicants. For instance, it had learned to penalise CVs that included words such as 'women' or references to women-only schools and universities.

Other recruitment algorithms have been known to discriminate against women with disabilities, for example by automatically evaluating their video interviews as substandard because of their facial expressions or the way they articulated sounds. Several incidents of this type have been documented over the last few years.

Finally, please be aware that you don't need a mortgage or job application to be exposed to the gendered side of algorithmic oppression. Here's a simple, rudimentary experiment that demonstrates this.

Have you ever played around with Google's auto-complete

function (i.e. the auto-filling system that suggests keywords linked to the ones you have just typed in)? If so, then you've also been interacting with an algorithm capable, in this case, of synthesising the millions of searches run on Google daily to lead us to the most 'relevant' results.

You could start, say, by typing into Google a phrase like 'a woman must'. While writing this book, I have done it more than once, on different dates and in different languages. With very slight differences, the auto-complete function spat back to me gems such as 'a woman must be submissive', a 'woman must never pursue a man' and 'a woman must give birth with pain'. When, instead, I wrote the keywords 'a man must', among Google's first seven suggestions there were 'a man must win over a woman's reluctance' and 'a man must not wear women's clothes'. As I tried out more 'creative' searches, things got even worse. 'Lesbians can' led to 'lesbians can become straight' and terms like 'African women' and 'Asian women' opened a Pandora's box filled with 'African women to order in marriage' and 'Asian women cost'. On more than one occasion, I had to restrain myself from kicking my laptop.

My little test has, of course, no scientific grounding, especially considering that Google varies its recommendations depending on the language in which you are writing, the place where you are typing from and your previous search history. But the thing is, I am by no means the only one to have had a go at this game. Sexist, racist and homophobic biases in Google auto-filling were at the centre of a recent UN Women campaign, have attracted the attention of journalists, engineers and AI experts, and continue to come up in specialised studies as well as in people's daily experiences.

The other point we should keep in mind is that misogynistic ways of thinking were not invented by an algorithm: if anything, they have long been ingrained in the worldview of many an algorithm user. The problem, though, is that Google does not simply register or catalogue such views. It keeps them alive, strengthening and spreading them, and ultimately helping inscribe them in the minds of its over four billion users across the planet.

Personally, I confess that every time I bump into maddening search suggestions, I think of my 18-year-old nephew (smart kid, crazy about all things digital, always with a smartphone in his hands) and my two nieces aged 9 and 7 (who in years to come will increasingly rely on Google for all sorts of tasks). And I cannot help but wonder what effects their generations will suffer due to the subliminal messages carried by algorithmic recommendations. Whenever it is deemed convenient, Google is perfectly able to intervene on its search algorithms, mostly by de-indexing problematic content (yet another issue we will soon come back to), it's just that it hardly seems to do it often enough.

So this is truly the crux of the matter: while most AI technology is not consciously designed with the purpose of distorting or marginalising, those who create or sell it often do very little to prevent this from happening. Which is why, in the remainder of this chapter, I will look more carefully at the decision-making processes in this area. Spoiler: I will pay special attention to those that are regularly excluded from key decisions and what their exclusion may mean for all of us.

* * *

Take the case of Timnit Gebru, colleague of and co-author with Joy Buolamwini, and an equally accomplished scientist and passionate advocate for digital justice.

Born and raised in Ethiopia, Timnit obtained political asylum in the USA, where she graduated at Stanford and worked first at Apple and then Google. In a short time, she became a legend in artificial intelligence circles and Google eventually entrusted to her its digital ethics team. In other words, whoever, globally, cared about the oppressive effects of algorithmic developments could legitimately look at Timnit as a spokesperson and a bad-ass problem-solver.

Timnit's success and credentials are even more impressive if we reflect on a few statistics. In the United States, where Timnit works and where a significant proportion of AI techniques are conceived or experimented with, only 3 per cent of informatics positions are occupied by African American women (less than 6 per cent go to their Asian colleagues and a mere 2 per cent to Latina professionals). These figures mirror, unfortunately, the startling under-representation of women, especially non-white, queer and disabled women, within the tech industry at the global level. Suffice it to say that a recent poll from programming community Stack Overflow found that out of 40,000 professional developers surveyed worldwide, less than 8 per cent are women and little more than 7 per cent are LGBTQ+ people. As for trans and disabled women, neither group reached two percentage points out of the total.

In case you are more interested in UK data, you should know that the stats are almost as depressing. Despite a promising influx of women in tech roles during the last five or six years, BCS, The Chartered Institute for IT, calculated in 2020 that women still made up only 20 per cent of the IT workforce. Even worse, Black women accounted for about 0.7 per cent of the sector, making their under-representation in digital arenas 2.5 times worse than it is for other industries.

This does not mean, of course, that across the globe there aren't excellent women technologists, many of whom are from a Black, Brown or queer background or have various types of disabilities, who are full of ideas on how to make digital innovation more inclusive and egalitarian. Still, the key issues are how these professionals, who already navigate a male-dominated and exclusionary world, are treated in the workplace, and whether or not there are real spaces for them to take up and exert influence. I operate in a different industry (academia) but have lost count of the times I have looked around the room and realised I was the only woman (or perhaps the only non-native English speaker, or the only non-British person). And trust me, it is not always easy to do your job when no one else looks or sounds the way you do.

But let's go back to Timnit Gebru, and to the work she did for Google. In 2020, Timnit was about to publish an examination of BERT, a language model that Google uses to process the subtleties of words and sentences typed in by users and to provide more accurate search results. In her article, however, Timnit argued that BERT was also the source of gender- and race-based discriminations and openly criticised its environmental impact (we often forget that powerful machines like those owned by Google need copious amounts of energy, which makes the tech industry one of the most polluting on the planet).

Alarmed by the international resonance those criticisms were likely to gain, Google demanded that the analysis be recanted, or, alternatively, for all names of co-authors associated with the firm to be removed. Timnit asked to know who had made that decision and declared herself ready to hand in her resignation should the company leadership refuse to discuss the matter further. In response to this, Google seems to have terminated her contract, insinuating, among other things, that Timnit's research was not up to date, having ignored a few improvements already introduced to mitigate the software's risks.

'It wasn't enough that they created a hostile work environment for people like me and [are building] products that are explicitly harmful to people in our community,' Timnit said after both the international press and many of her former colleagues had started to make noise around her departure. 'It's not enough that they don't listen when you say something. Then they try to silence your scientific voice.' To this day, Google's version of the story is that Timnit wasn't fired but chose to resign.

After parting ways with Google – you might be curious to hear – Timnit has not taken on any other corporate position and has kept busy founding a study centre on digital ethics, the Distributed Artificial Intelligence Research Institute. The institute's board is packed with women, LGBTQ+ individuals and people of colour, who all combine technical expertise with an activist outlook. I warmly recommend you go and scroll their profiles and latest research, which provide us with a much-needed ray of hope.

Going back to our broader analysis of the tech industry's decision-making processes, though, many questions are still left unanswered. We are left to wonder, for example, how Google executives could live with letting go such a bright mind, or why a corporation with the mantra of 'openness' and 'corporate responsibility' seemed unable to take on board frank criticisms on the risks of algorithmic bias.

Worst of all, as you have probably gathered, Timnit's case is not an isolated one. And the web of injustices behind her story is way bigger than the misconduct or the pettiness of any individual tech giant.

* * *

Before drawing any conclusions, you may want to consider a few other examples, all connected to companies currently producing or utilising questionable AI technologies.

Let us start with Amazon, one of the world's richest companies, as well as a major producer of cutting-edge algorithmic technology. Do you remember their 'sexist' recruitment software? Precisely for this reason, you might be interested to learn that Jeff Bezos's multinational is currently dealing with an avalanche of workplace harassment lawsuits, a great number of which have been filed by women of colour and sexual minority women.

One of them, African American Charlotte Newman, who took her case to court in 2022, subsequently declared that while at Amazon she has been denied promotions, offered roles that did not reflect her qualifications, and has received sexist and racist comments from her superiors. Predictably enough, the firm has claimed to be 'conducting thorough investigations' and said that it was 'working hard to foster a diverse, equitable and inclusive culture'. Yet only a few months later, the management had to face no fewer than five new litigations: four initiated by women of colour (two Black employees, one Latina and one Asian) and one by a lesbian woman. One of the complainants reported having been called the n-word by her boss after disconnecting too rapidly from a video call. Another explained she was called a 'bitch', an 'idiot' and a 'nobody' by white male managers. And an African American colleague of theirs, who did not join the lawsuits but talked anonymously to the press, said that her supervisor assured her she should trust him because, well, his ancestors 'owned slaves, but he was pretty sure they were good to them'. At the time of publication the lawsuits are ongoing.

Furthermore, pretty much at the same time, an equality and diversity expert named Chanin Kelly-Rae, who had been hired by Amazon with the specific purpose of preventing incidents like the ones I just described, resigned less than a year after the beginning of her contract. Chanin (also an African American) declared she had simply realised the company had no real intention of listening to her and that 'Amazon appeared to be taking steps backward instead of forward'. She also added that she had been contacted, both during her tenure and after leaving Amazon, by flocks of ex-employees, who told her of how they had suffered extreme anxiety, night terrors and even spontaneous miscarriages as a result of the stress faced during their time with the corporation.

So there we are, right back where we started from: contemplating the many vicious circles triggered by patriarchal digital capitalism. And, in this instance, it is one vicious circle in particular: the one that connects the abuse and the prejudices amplified by digital technologies to the prejudices and the abuse inflicted on the brave women who seek to make things better.

Let's put it like this: if female employees have to spend their working days defending themselves from harassment and toxic working conditions, can we expect them to channel their energy into making technology fairer and more egalitarian? And if the tech industry pushes away women like Chanin Kelly-Rae, missing out on the expertise of professionals who could improve the state of the sector, can we truly envisage revolutionary changes in the near future?

Unfortunately, it is the same old story when we turn our attention back to Google.

Some of you may perhaps remember the 'Google women's walkout' of a few years ago. Should you not, allow me to refresh your memory. Had you entered one of Google's offices around the world on 1 November 2018 you would have found most of them nearly empty, all desks covered in notes that read: 'I'm not at my desk because I'm walking out in solidarity with other Googlers and contractors to protest [against] sexual harassment, misconduct, lack of transparency and a workplace culture that's not working for everyone.' Outside some of the offices, you would have found a lot of very angry employees, some of them holding signs saying: 'What do I do at Google? I work hard every day so the company can afford $90,000,000 payouts to execs who sexually harass my co-workers'.

What Google's women (and their many sympathetic male colleagues) were rebelling against was the cover-up of a sequence of instances of sexual harassment within the company. Not long before, the *New York Times* had published an explosive article, revealing that the Californian giant's former vice president, Andy Rubin, had been accused by a female employee of forcing her into a sexual relationship. While being asked to leave, Rubin had reportedly been offered a severance package worth tens of millions of dollars, with Google burying the real reasons behind his departure. And that was the proverbial straw that broke the camel's back.

Over the following months, the strike attracted much international support, forcing the corporation to take under consideration a few of the protesters' requests (among others, more transparent and efficient mechanisms to report sexual misconduct and a stronger focus on the danger of algorithmic distortions). Nonetheless, as shown by Timnit Gebru's vicissitudes, we can't truly say that the company leadership has kept its promises.

There is more. We already got a glimpse of Uber's workplace culture when examining the firm's treatment of trans drivers like Janey Webb. Yet a closer look at Uber's history reveals that cases like Janey's are only the tip of the iceberg.

In 2017, Uber's co-founder and then CEO Travis Kalanick was forced to resign after one of his former engineers, Susan Fowler, had exposed the culture of sexism and inequality that reigned in his business.

Before leaving Uber, Susan had reported in vain to human resources several flagrant disparities in treatment she and her female colleagues had encountered, such as insults, unwanted sexual propositions and gender-based discriminations in promotions and benefits. She had also noted how this heavy atmosphere had prompted most women employees (already a small minority within the firm) to quit their positions. Perhaps the most scandalous of these incidents had taken place on Susan's first day of work, when a manager had overtly approached her for sex. She had correctly reported him to human resources, providing them with copies of all the inappropriate messages he had sent to her. HR got back to her saying that, even though what had happened certainly qualified as sexual harassment, this was the guy's first offence and the company executives did not feel like punishing him with more than a verbal reprimand.

'Over the next few months, I began to meet more women

engineers in the company. As I got to know them, and heard their stories, I was surprised that some of them had stories similar to my own,' Susan wrote in a blog published after resigning from her post. 'Some of the women even had stories about reporting the exact same manager I had reported, and had reported inappropriate interactions with him long before I had even joined the company. It became obvious that both HR and management had been lying about this being "his first offense", and it certainly wasn't his last. [...] The situation was escalated as far up the chain as it could be escalated, and still nothing was done.'

If the beginning of Susan's story has made your hackles rise (that is certainly the effect it had on me), I bet you'll find its end quite bittersweet. Susan's blog, in fact, rapidly went viral and was then reshared by global media, which led to an internal investigation that shook Uber's leadership to its foundations. Even though the company did its best to disprove and counteract her accusations, not only the CEO but also several other executives were eventually forced to resign. Next, Susan was rightfully celebrated as the initiator of the 'tech industry's #MeToo' and was even featured on the cover of *Time* magazine, for which she now authors a regular column. Still, Uber continues to be in the eye of the storm due to its treatment of women employees, customers and gig workers. And the rest of the digital sector – including many businesses developing algorithmic mechanisms – remains rife with systemic harassment.

For further confirmation that what happened at Google, Amazon and Uber is not merely anecdotical evidence, I recommend browsing a recent publication from think tank Women Who Tech (see page 212). Out of a sample of more than 1,000 women active in the tech industry, the organisation calculated that 44 per cent had been the object of unwanted sexual attention, groping and verbal offences. Among the testimonies collected by the researchers, there were stories of rapes and other violent physical assaults and – once again – accounts suggesting that queer, non-white and minority women are even more at risk.

I have to confess that as I skimmed through such disheartening figures there was one fact that stuck with me most of all. Today's sexual harassment stats remain nearly identical to those of 2017–18, when, after Susan Fowler's revelations and the Google women's walkout, Big Tech leaders swore to anyone willing to listen that they were going to tackle sexism and sexual misconduct within the industry.

So let's just say it once and for all. There is a deep-rooted misogynistic underbelly that permeates the digital sector in its entirety – an underbelly that is directly connected to the development of problematic technologies. Because what stories such as Timnit Gebru's, Chanin Kelly-Rae's and Susan Fowler's demonstrate is that there are, most certainly, women willing to make tech companies accountable and to increase their sensitivity to the ethcial side of technology. But these change-makers have more than one enemy to battle against.

* * *

Academics studying the ethical dimension of innovation have long hung on to a famous aphorism, saying that no technology is good or bad, but, at the same time, no technology is truly neutral. This seemingly contradictory statement is very close to my heart, since it captures two fundamental aspects of the problem. First, it reminds us that practically any technology can be used to perpetrate violence or exclusion. And second, it suggests that because technologies are created by human beings, the errors, the distortions and the not always noble goals typical of any human mind are often *encoded* into them.

Now, it seems to me that these reflections are even more urgent in a capitalistic and patriarchal society, where technology development is largely controlled by a few elite organisations, which, in turn, are dominated by (mostly white, heterosexual and otherwise privileged) men. Incidentally, as has been observed by many feminist analysts before me, already in centuries past men's dominance over both the economy and technology resulted in the domination of specific 'masculine' kinds of machines. For example, who do you think we have to thank for the invention and the proliferation of all kinds of guns, tanks and bombs? Obviously, legions and legions of men. We must admit, however, that the digital revolution has infused this old dynamic with new life.

The stories of transgender Uber drivers and of African American mortgage applicants in particular should provide us with a timely alert. Perhaps even more than other technologies, these AI tools are generally viewed as objective and infallible. Yet we have already seen how they are anything but neutral and how, instead, they risk replicating and magnifying the mistakes and the biases of their developers and their users, alongside the prejudices of societies at large.

Nor does this apply only to facial-recognition tools, Google searches or recruitment and credit algorithms. Software able to discriminate on the bases of gender and other sensitive characteristics is currently used to allocate welfare benefits and social housing, as well as in medical research. This is precisely why those entrusted with the design and functioning of algorithmic tools should not only be a demographically heterogenous group, but also be aware of the impact of digital advancements on inequalities. Except this is exactly where the vicious circle effect starts to kick in.

On the one hand, women and other historically oppressed people are massively under-represented in the decision-making bodies of the tech industry. On the other hand, whenever talented professionals like Timnit Gebru and her many fellow 'troublemakers' challenge this, that very same industry obstructs them, ostracises them and at times even forces them to quit their jobs. So, the bottom line: the ecosystem continues to produce controversial tools and turns them into profit.

And the circle has its own internal logic. Should it come as a surprise that organisations controlled by the dominant groups within capitalist and patriarchal society develop technologies that pay little attention to the needs of people who have always been in a subordinate position? Should it come as a surprise that the same management establishments allowing their digital experts to be regularly harassed do not take seriously the complaints of other, more vulnerable employees, such as trans gig worker Janey Webb? (For we already know, having looked at the plight of online content moderators, that women might be scarce at the top of the tech industry ladder, but there are plenty of them at the very bottom.)

No matter which way we look at it, it is not hard to spot how the mechanism works or to appreciate that it adds another piece to our analysis, from which the digital revolution starts emerging as an undemocratic, unequitable phenomenon that leaves an indelible mark on women's lives.

CHAPTER 3

The bodies behind the screen

Content warning

This chapter contains specific details of incidents of sexual violence.

'My rapists put me in a mental prison all on their own, but it is Pornhub who gave me a life sentence and threw away the key,' wrote then 26-year-old indigenous activist Rose Kalemba in a witness statement that gives me goosebumps every single time I go through it. She addressed those words to a Canadian parliamentary committee that had just launched a pioneering study into the practices of several digital platforms, among them the largest porn-sharing site on the planet: Canadian-owned Pornhub.

In 2009, Rose, who was 14 years old, was abducted by two men, who beat her up, stabbed her and sexually assaulted her for over 12 hours. The rapists filmed themselves and shortly after posted the footage on Pornhub. There were six videos in total, all with a download option next to them, allowing viewers to save them on their computers and share them elsewhere. Associated taglines included: 'teen crying and getting slapped around', 'teen getting destroyed' and 'passed out teen'.

Once the images were posted online, people Rose knew started to recognise her and personal details like her full name, age, school and home address were soon leaked on the channel's comments section. From day one – Rose explained to the Canadian lawmakers – she begged Pornhub to delete the films, warning them it portrayed the violent rape of a teenage girl. But the company allegedly chose to ignore her frantic appeals and the videos were left online for at least six months. 'Every single day I had to watch the view counts continue to rise, while ads appeared along with the rape videos. The number of views eventually exceeded 2 million,' Rose wrote in a written statement that has been subsequently made publicly available. On more than one occasion, this re-victimisation led Rose to consider suicide. As a last resort, she contacted Pornhub again, this time pretending to be a lawyer and threatening legal action. It appears the videos were then removed within 48 hours.

By this point, however, the images had travelled too far already, getting lost in the Web and becoming nearly impossible to delete. Many Internet users had kept copies of Rose's assault and some even tried to blackmail her, threatening to repost shots of their 'favourite moments'.

'None of my attempts to stay out of the public eye and "start over" over all these years has ever worked,' Rose explained, 'there was always someone who found me and would harass me, share my updated personal information online.' Tired of 'waking up every day praying that one more person wouldn't recognize me as "THAT" girl', she decided to waive her right to anonymity and publicly told her story in a blog that was rapidly picked up by the BBC and other international media.

Pornhub was never able to provide a credible account of what happened to Rose. Questioned by the Standing Committee on Access to Information, Privacy and Ethics, one of Pornhub's at-that-time proprietors, David Tassillo, declared that he would have to 'go back and verify the exact timeline' and that there might have been a record of Rose's correspondence with the platform, but 'well, we [Pornhub] do have an email retention time'. His business partner, Feras Antoon, was equally unable to provide accurate information, both on Rose's incident and on other instances of non-consensual pornography connected with Pornhub. Still, he specified those events made him 'sad', since he was 'a father' and he had 'a daughter', 'a wife', 'a mother'. I really do not understand why men implicated in sexual misconduct cases always mention their daughters, their female partners and their mothers.

For women like Rose, though, sharing their story on their own terms feels like taking back some of their power. Rose herself has explained that she found strength in the knowledge that as an indigenous woman speaking up was even more necessary. She knew only too well that her fellow indigenous women are dramatically exposed to gender-based violence. 'I don't want what happened to me and so many other women, girls and two spirit people before me to become synonymous with being indigenous,' she wrote in her testimony. 'I want better for my people.'

It is thanks to contributions like Rose's that Canadian legislators have eventually recommended urgent measures against platforms like Pornhub. It is also entirely thanks to those contributions that millions of people have finally started to grasp what hides behind the reassuring facade of the 'friendly' giant of online porn.

* * *

For those not in the know, Pornhub is the world's main pornographic portal. It was founded in Canada in 2007 and since then it has grown in size and profits at a frankly astonishing pace. In 2019, it reached 115 million daily visits, making for a total of 42 billion visits per year. For several years, the platform has successfully portrayed itself as the naughty but socially responsible face of both online porn and social media and invested a great deal in social-washing initiatives. It has contributed funds to environmental causes and made donations to breast cancer research for every view in its 'big tit' and 'small tit' video categories. At the beginning of the Covid-19 pandemic, it even offered free access to its premium version in countries in lockdown.

Not all that glitters is gold, though.

First of all, it is helpful to know that Pornhub is owned by an unobtrusively named, cleverly marketed business called MindGeek. This corporation claims on its website to be trading in 'search engine optimization' and 'web advertising' services. In reality, it owns not only Pornhub, but about ten other adult websites (among them RedTube and YouPorn, also some of the biggest and most visited globally). Lately, thanks to a combination of subscriptions and advertisement, it has cashed in about $460 million per year.

Many of MindGeek's services, in essence, work like YouTubes of porn (porn tubes), in the sense that they allow users both to watch and to post explicit materials, many of which are amateur videos. These spontaneous uploads have drastically cut the platforms' production costs, enabling MindGeek to establish a de facto monopoly on the world's pornographic offering. In so doing, the corporation has put out of business many smaller and alternative adult film producers. Ethical and feminist-friendly porn is expensive to create: as a minimum requirement, fully consenting adult actors need to be paid and their safety must be contractually guaranteed.

MindGeek has huge responsibilities towards women and girls like Rose Kalemba and I'll now explain why this is the case.

On paper, all of MindGeek's platforms ban both child pornography and any other form of non-consensual content. In practice, tubes like Pornhub do contain this type of material. In 2019, *Sunday Times* reporters found hundreds of such videos on the site, some left on the platform for over three years. The British charity Internet Watch Foundation identified 118 images of child rape uploaded on the platform in the same period.

Every country has its victims and survivors, and their tales are not an easy read. In America, another young teenager, Serena Fleites, was still in school when her then boyfriend pressured her into shooting an explicit video, which was then circulated between her peers and eventually uploaded on to Pornhub. Serena was also heard by Ottawa's Standing Committee, and together with other young women she is suing Pornhub. In her lawsuit she explains that she spent weeks trying to get her video taken down, only to see it being repeatedly re-uploaded.

Another court case involving Pornhub was prompted by the accusations of a group of women whom a company called Girls Do Porn lured into a studio inviting them to a fashion shoot and they were then manipulated into performing sex on camera. After those scenes were posted on Girls Do Porn's channel on Pornhub, Girls Do

Porn's proprietor was ordered to pay the plaintiffs very substantial compensation. Nonetheless, some of the clips remained available on Pornhub for a few days after the verdict. Similarly, although MindGeek prides itself on being a 'supporter' and 'protector' of sex workers (many of whom use its sites to make ends meet), it is, once again, on Pornhub that videos stolen from adult performers have often ended up in recent years.[2]

Now, let me be clear on one thing. Porn tubes are not the only outlets for footage like Rose's and Serena's. In the 2000s and 2010s, for example, tellingly titled sites such as MyEx, Expic and My Fucking Ex-Girlfriend blossomed in different countries. They invited anonymous users to submit nude photos of their exes as an act of revenge and then monetised the uploads through advertisement.

The most notorious of these websites was probably IsAnyOneUp, founded in 2010 by a dark-eyed, flamboyant Californian named Hunter Moore, who liked calling himself a 'professional life-ruiner'. The BBC refer to people calling him 'the Net's most hated man', a title which he also claimed as a badge of honour. Hunter's portal had, in fact, a peculiarity: posters were required to upload, together with the unaware victims' explicit images, their full name, home address, work address and a screenshot of their social media profiles (an abusive practice known as doxing). Once 'named and shamed',

2   Even leaving aside non-consensual pornography, the relationship between sex work and porn tubes is rather complex and probably deserves a book of its own. That said, it is helpful to know that many sex workers use these platforms and ask for their needs to be taken into account when new legislation on online pornography is considered. Not being able to do justice to this debate, I have included some relevant sources in the References.

many women submitted to IsAnyOneUp had their nudes sent to their parents, their new partners or their employers. Some lost their jobs, others were ostracised by conservative family members and many developed mental health problems.

Harrowingly, however, not only did the owners of these sites care very little for the misery they created, they saw it as a business opportunity. 'I do not want anybody to ever be hurt by my site – physically. I don't give a fuck about emotionally. Deal with it,' Hunter Moore once said to an extremely bewildered journalist. He even added: 'If somebody killed themselves over that? Do you know how much money I'd make? At the end of the day, I do not want anybody to hurt themselves. But if they do? Thank you for the money.'

Money was certainly there to be made. IsAnyOneUp remained online for 16 months, after which it was shut down due to fear of lawsuits and personal retaliations. During the time it was online it reportedly received a total of 30 million site visits, earning up to $13,000 per month in advertisements.

That being said, platforms like Hunter Moore's remain a relatively small fish in the gigantic pond that is the global supply of online porn. Furthermore, thanks to the anti-digital violence laws which are gradually being passed in many countries, judicial authorities manage most of the time to ultimately shut them down. Porn tubes, on the other hand, are a very different story, in terms of both longevity and reach.

For a start, it is worth noticing that portals like those owned by MindGeek host such a jaw-dropping quantity of amateur videos that very little control can actually be exerted on their nature. As a result, images such as Rose Kalemba's may remain online for months or years, or at least for long enough to get lost in a labyrinth of cross-shares and downloads.

What is more, many of MindGeek's sites use algorithmic techniques as sophisticated as those employed by Facebook and Google, which are leveraged to extract from users a bonanza of information. By analysing user data (the porn searched for, the videos watched for the most amount of time, the preferences of people from similar demographics) the tubes can then offer their visitors a uniquely refined offering, tailored to individual predilections. MindGeek's goal, of course, is to keep them online for as long as possible, maximising its profits, but this strategy has an enormous impact on stories such as Rose's.

Every time a Pornhub user watched the videos of Rose's rape, Pornhub's algorithm registered it. In time, it then redirected that person (or perhaps another person of the same age, or, say, from the same geographical region or a similar demographic group) towards similar videos: namely, extremely violent, amateurish-looking films, portraying very young-looking teenagers. So let's just pause and consider the mind-blowing ramifications of this mechanism.

First, the circulation of videos like Rose's on sites as big and popular as Pornhub has dramatically increased the demand for analogous content (suffice it to say that 'real rape' have become rather common search words on both Google and adult portals). Second, many professional producers now wish to satisfy this burgeoning demand and have started to give their products an increasingly amateurish look. This means it has become even harder to check the origins of the porn that is online and to distinguish non-consensual footage and even real-life images of rapes from studio-made films.

How do MindGeek executives react to this perverse cycle (yet another one within patriarchal digital capitalism)? A short but honest answer is: in the exact same way other digital companies I have already discussed deal with their own corporate image problems. That is to say, at first with indifference, and then they try to cut their losses once public pressure appears unsustainable.

The parliamentary study Rose Kalemba and Serena Fleites contributed to, in particular, has caused MindGeek huge PR difficulties. Since then, Pornhub has been forced to cancel thousands and thousands of videos and to introduce new moderation procedures and policies limiting users' ability to download and post videos without age or identity checks. Xtube, a smaller site owned by the same group, has also recently shut down and, as I write, while staying on in a shareholder capacity, Feras Antoon and David Tassillo have been forced to resign from the company leadership. But MindGeek has other functioning portals and many other companies have copied its business model.

This is why I'm now going to ask you once again to look beyond the malpractices of any single corporation. In the second half of this chapter, in fact, we will investigate in depth a broader, time-honoured capitalist tradition: turning women's bodies and sexual intimacy into a cash cow – needless to say, without asking for their permission.

* * *

About a year before Rose Kalemba, another woman was raped. Once again this savagery ended up being monetised – although perhaps less directly – by the global tech industry.

The woman's name was Mirindi Euprazi. At the time she was 50 years old and lived with her husband and four teenage children (a son and three daughters) in a village named Ninja, in the Democratic Republic of the Congo (DRC). The DRC is filled with precious minerals such as gold, cobalt, tungsten and, above all, coltan, or tantalum, all essential to the functioning of electronic gadgets such as tablets and smartphones. Since the 1990s, the entire region has been marked by bloody armed conflicts, where multiple factions attempted to seize control of these highly profitable mineral reserves or used them to fund their military activities.

One day an armed militia entered Mirindi's house and raped her in front of her husband, before killing him on the spot. Next, the soldiers forced Mirindi's teenage son to have sex with her and afterwards they murdered him too. They left after having robbed her of all her possessions and took with them her 13-, 14- and 17-year-old daughters. When, months later, Mirindi's testimony was collected by a nurse and then reported in the *Guardian*, she had no news of any of them.

Mirindi is one of the hundred of thousands of women, aged between 1 and 90 years old, systematically brutalised in the DRC over the last 30 years, as part of wars often connected, as I mentioned above, to the exploitation of mineral reserves.

The phenomenon has complicated causes and multifarious implications, and it is hard to quantify its exact proportions. The United Nations calculated, however, that from 1998 onwards at least 200,000 rapes have been perpetrated by both armed factions and the Congolese national army, and the estimate is regarded as a conservative one. According to several studies, these aggressions have been used as a war strategy, a method to seize control of occupied territories and subjugate local populations, and even as a way to train male soldiers, often recruited as adolescents and exposed themselves to ferocious abuse.

You should know that in the meantime, corporations such as Apple, Sony, Toshiba and Samsung have all utilised minerals linked to these conflicts and this violence. Starting from the 2000s, the vicissitudes of Congolese women have gradually started to attract lots of international attention. Gold, tungsten and tantalum have therefore been declared 'conflict minerals' and a few legal reforms in the USA and the EU have partially regulated their use within the tech industry. This, however, stopped neither the brutalities nor the economic exploitation.

In 2017–18, for instance, Médecins Sans Frontières assisted and interviewed thousands of women in the DRC's province of Kananga. One of them, Cécile (pseudonym), had been attacked not long before by men armed with tear gas.

'I was at home with my husband that day. It was during the violence and fighting. We heard screams outside and neighbours crying,' she told the doctors, describing to them how eight men had eventually forced themselves into their home. 'They threatened to kill my husband and tried to force him to rape our daughter. She was 17. He refused and they murdered him. Then they raped our daughter, and me. When they left, I hid in the forest next to the village with my children. I didn't sleep or eat.'

Another Kananga resident, Mamie (pseudonym), witnessed the murder of three of her five children, and the girls were raped before they were killed. 'I was at home when armed men came and killed my husband. They decapitated him and stole all our possessions. I was raped in my home, next to my husband's body, in the presence of my children. […] They stole all our belongings, they took everything. Then they forced us out, without giving me time to get dressed. I was naked from the waist up.'

Mamie also explained how she miraculously survived. 'I just grabbed something to cover my chest as we were chased out of our home. I started walking with my two children through the bush to Tshikapa. I didn't know where we were going, I just started walking. […] Again, they raped us. There were three of them. After that we hid so as not to be raped again.' When she sought treatment at the Médecins Sans Frontières' hospital, Mamie discovered she had also contracted HIV – a relatively common occurrence among rape survivors in the area.

Women like Mirindi, Mamie and Cécile often arrive in hospital unable to walk or speak. Some avoid returning to their villages out of fear they'll be attacked again. The younger ones might not disclose what has happened to them, worrying they might be unable to find a husband or be repudiated by their spouses. However, you will be relieved to learn that many undergo extraordinary, albeit daunting, healing journeys in rescue centres founded by fellow Congolese women and their national and international supporters. Among these indefatigable activists are human rights activist Christine Schuler Deschryver, co-founder and director of the recovery centre City of Joy, and gynaecologist Dr Denis Mukwege, who in 2018 was awarded the Nobel Peace Prize for treating thousands of DRC's rape survivors.

Meanwhile, however, many tech companies continue to use in their supply chains minerals whose extraction is linked to armed groups or violence in the region. The suffering that the mineral trade brings about is such that many Congolese women wish they had been born in a country poorer in natural resources and less tightly connected to the digital revolution. 'I wish we had no gold and no other minerals,' said a 24-year-old Congolese woman to a UK journalist. 'I just want peace and my husband back, that's all.'

* * *

About two years ago, I went with one of my best friends, Francesca, to hear Dr Denis Mukwege speak; he'd come to London for a series of public events. Given his tireless commitment to the care of his patients, he is nicknamed 'the doctor who mends women'. I don't think I'll ever forget his description of a woman he had once operated on. She hadn't only been raped: they had also shot her between her legs.

What stuck with me from Dr Mukwege's speech was the clarity with which he unmasked the economic interests behind the assault on Congolese women. He told us that 'without the DRC's tantalum, computers and mobile phones all over the world couldn't work' and that 'all the conflicts where women's bodies are used as a battlefield are motivated by the same goal: pushing populations out of their villages, creating lawless territories, and appropriating this mineral to sell it on international markets.'

The Nobel prize-winner reminded us that following the digital revolution the great capitalist machine has come up with more than one new way to profit from sexual violence. As we have seen, new technologies have made it possible to monetise rape by simply filming it and posting it online (and, incidentally, by endlessly re-victimising rape survivors like Rose Kalemba), but technology production is also linked to different and somewhat more traditional forms of sexual exploitation. The truth is, there is barely any electronic gadget that can function without raw materials extracted and laboured away from Western countries. And the systematic violation of women's bodies has tragically become just another means to gain control over such resources.

In a packed lecture theatre, where you could have cut the tension with a knife, Denis Mukwege also spoke to us of the activism of his countrywomen, many of whom are themselves rape survivors, and who fight to make the DRC a safer place for women and for all. To those who ask him about his views on the legislation adopted on conflict minerals in Europe and North America, the doctor said bluntly that these laws are still totally insufficient to clean up our gadgets' supply chain. And to be fair, it is hard to contradict him.

Attempts to date to regulate the use of the DRC's minerals in the tech industry have produced unforeseen and paradoxical outcomes. For one thing, the reforms have obliged digital companies to conduct due diligence checks and to demonstrate that no armed group benefits from transactions they are involved with. The problem is that these control procedures have also delayed extraction operations, causing many job losses and at times pushing starving miners straight into the arms of the militias.

Plus, there are many ways to bypass current regulations. A 2019 report from the Danish Institute for International Studies, for example, established that even after the new laws became effective about 200 of the DRC's extraction sites remain under the indirect influence of armed groups. While not always controlling them directly, the militias may tax their profits or own some of their shares. Meanwhile, the United Nations has continued to document sexual violence outbreaks on a large scale in various areas of the country.

Finally, there is clear evidence of further injustices suffered by the Congolese women participating in mining activities.

'I'm not healthy because I have to pound rocks and carry the heavy sacks at the mines. I've become weak and have lost weight. I came here as a refugee because there's food here,' said a 25-year-old woman named Yvonne Starko to the *Guardian*. She had fled her village to protect herself from rape and had since then been forced to work as a miner to feed her children. At Yvonne's mine, they extract cassiterite, another mineral used in mobile phone circuit boards. And as reported by international labour rights charities, female workers in the area can be paid less than a dollar a day and are generally given the hardest and lowest-paid tasks, which at times they are physically unable to carry out. In order to get a job, many of them are also forced to sleep with the mines' owners.

Different extraction sites seem to have different problems. Cobalt pits, among others, have recently been much talked about by the press, since miners' hazardous working conditions and their continuous exposure to cobalt dust have been associated with breathing difficulties and even fatal lung disease. Women, specifically, were reported to carry on their backs cobalt sacks as heavy as 50 kilograms.

Just like cassiterite and tantalum, cobalt is essential to the tech industry: you'll find it in most electronic equipment with a lithium rechargeable battery. Unlike the other two minerals, however, it is not considered a 'conflict mineral', which, according to several human rights researchers, explains why supply chain controls in this field seem to be even less tight than in others.

Things are no better in gold and tantalum mines. A woman called Mireille Mbale, who works in one of them, told US non-profit Women's Media Center that in her workplace 'the woman is treated like a thing' and is 'insulted and neglected'. Amnesty International believes that these extraction sites employ boys and girls under the age of ten and that female miners (many of whom have a history of surviving wartime rapes) are subjected to constant sexual harassment.

Simply put, the problem doesn't end with armed militias. It lies, instead, with the exploitation and violence pervading the industry as a whole.

'The heart of the matter is that the current laws only control the last step of the supply chain: the purchase of minerals that end up in our phones. But they don't really intervene on the entire economic system,' were, not without reason, Denis Mukwege's last words on that night a couple of years ago.

Francesca and I could not help but stare uncomfortably at the smartphones in our handbags.

* * *

I am aware that in this chapter I have shared some dreadful stories, which – I confess – I have struggled to write up. Some of Rose Kalemba's words, for example, got embedded in my mind so deeply that when I was writing of her case I could not sleep at night. When I started to research mass rapes in the DRC and read testimonies such as Mirindi's, Mamie's and Cécile's, I often burst into tears in front of the screen, my eyes full of gut-wrenching scenes. Nonetheless, I am convinced these stories need to be part of the discussion. Firstly, because what happened to these women *cannot* and *must not* be forgotten. And secondly, if we want to do right by these sisters of ours the least we can do is have a proper look at the tangle of economic interests and misogynistic power that lies behind their stories.

At least initially, I suppose you might have asked yourself: *What on earth has non-consensual pornography got to do with war rapes in the DRC?* The answer is that the experiences of Jess Phillips MP and content moderator Isabella Plunkett, and those of trans driver Janey Webb and AI computer scientist Timnit Gebru are all held together by an invisible thread, and that thread is, naturally, the destructive relationship between capitalism, patriarchy and technology.

Mind you, we are facing a problem that is at once very old and very new. For centuries, women have been assaulted to generate profit: just to state the obvious, war rapes, sexual slavery and sex trafficking all prospered well before the advent of market economies. (Patriarchy, let us not forget, is much, much older than capitalism.) During the last five centuries, however, the patriarchal and the capitalistic logics have continued to support one another, with sexual violence being used to build actual economic empires. Just think of the role played by millions of Black women slaves in the construction of the American economy. Slaves who were not only forced to work in the fields, but also turned into sexual and reproductive machines. Slaves whose bodies and children were treated merely as things that belonged directly to their masters.

Today, fortunately, the vast majority of the world regards sexual abuse and its monetisation as an obscene violation of women's human rights. Still, this scourge has not disappeared. From the women who get raped to seize coltan mines, to the female miners who must keep up with the sexual blackmail of their bosses, to the girls whose privacy is desecrated online, sexual exploitation and brutality are omnipresent along the digital supply chain.

While these aspects are different from one another, it is vital that we piece them all together. So let me be clear. We should certainly be outraged at the non-consensual sex scenes just a couple of clicks away on our tablets – this is an intolerable plight brought about by the digital revolution. But we should equally be mindful of what goes on in the factories where those tablets are produced (remember Tian Yu and her Foxconn assembly line?) and in the extraction site of the minerals that make them function. Gender injustice is rampant at all levels of technology production, except even those of us who closely follow technology developments tend to focus mostly on its immaterial aspects (namely, on online interactions), forgetting that the digital economy has a side that is more *material* than ever.

In this book's first part, I have tried to remedy this short-sightedness by shedding light on the many vicious circles typical of patriarchal digital capitalism.

I will now explore this ecosystem in even further depth in the next part of the book. I will look at very disparate issues: at how business models popular within the tech industry favour misogynistic violence; at new forms of exploitative work introduced by the digital revolution; at the way all this evolved during the Covid-19 pandemic; and at the relationship between tech and politics. I do promise you, however, that this broader analysis will still be guided by the very same conviction: that existing injustices must be unveiled one by one if our hope is to finally change direction.

PART 2

Technology, patriarchy and capitalism

CHAPTER 4

The cyber rape market

Tiziana Cantone was 32 when she unwillingly became an online sensation. Born in a small village near Naples, she had a loving mother, a pair of gorgeous eyes and a rocky relationship with an older man, Sergio Di Palo.

In April 2015, she sent to him and to four more recipients some videos that showed her having sex with a number of men. To this day, it remains unclear how wholeheartedly Tiziana had agreed to perform sexual acts on camera – while the recordings display no sign of coercion, her family argues that her boyfriend enjoyed seeing her with others and manipulated her into fulfilling this fantasy. How exactly the clips came to be circulated beyond those initial exchanges is also a mystery. But by the time a friend rang Tiziana to say the films had popped up on an adult website it was already too late.

Within weeks, the footage was being shared all over Italian WhatsApp chats and European and US adult portals, with a phrase the young woman was heard speaking in one of the scenes ('You're filming? Bravo!') becoming a popular Internet meme. Tiziana's words were parodied by songwriters and footballers on YouTube, and printed on T-shirts and smartphone covers sold on eBay. They also went viral on Facebook, which filled up with fake profiles named after her, Photoshopped pictures of her face and satirical pages created with the sole purpose of vilifying her.

Like Tiziana, I, too, am a Neapolitan thirtysomething. Still today, I vividly remember how someone who could have been a friend of mine all of a sudden became the talk of the town. I also remember how her Southern Italian origins were an important part of the story. The Web was rife with impressions of her accent, making her an object of both ridicule and fetishisation. People spoke of her as a 'Neapolitan whore', and renowned Northern Italian journalists mocked her using words in Southern dialect.

Yes, renowned journalists. Because while Tiziana's existence turned into a living hell, the Italian press treated her as a cultural phenomenon. Local news sites interviewed passers-by in her home town asking what they thought of the videos and whether they knew the woman appearing in them. National newspapers reported her full name and her identifying details. As a result the clips, by then available via Google searches as basic as 'tiziana cantone hot video', rapidly reached almost one million views.

Rape and death threats flooded Tiziana's mailbox and people began to recognise her on the street. She quit her job, started proceedings to change her name and went into hiding in another region. Determined to regain control of her life, she ultimately took legal action to get all the videos and comments removed from the Internet.

Considering the torture she was being subjected to, the account Tiziana gave to Italian public prosecutors was admirably clear. She explained she had willingly shot the videos, but had never authorised their large-scale distribution.

'I want justice,' said Tiziana to the magistrates. 'I am asking for my videos to be taken down from these sites that are devastating my life.' By 'these sites' she was referring to Facebook, Google, YouTube and a few other platforms, all explicitly mentioned in the lawsuit.

It took until August 2016 for a Neapolitan court to recognise Tiziana's right to have all her images, links to her videos and obscene comments deleted from Facebook, but not from Google-owned YouTube, which was acquitted due to clerical errors made by Tiziana's solicitor. Moreover, the judges rejected her request to have links to her private materials – videos, references to her name, identifying details as well as the abusive comments – deleted from Google search results. Their reasoning was that Tiziana's story was still 'of public interest' and that a search engine could not, in any case, be held responsible for simply indexing what had been shared on other websites. To add insult to injury, Tiziana was ordered to pay a total of €20,000 in legal expenses.

A few weeks passed, after which Tiziana's aunt found her dead in the basement of her house, hanging on a blue silk scarf.

Tiziana's mother, Maria Teresa Giglio, has since then devoted herself to the defence of her daughter's memory and to shedding light on what actually happened to her. 'Words are barely enough to describe what [Tiziana] had to suffer, and what she suffers to this day, since she is still called unspeakable names, and her memory continues to be desecrated. Her shaming seems to have no end,' were her exact words in a recent autobiography.

To this day, Italian investigators are trying to ascertain whether Tiziana's death might have been a suicide or a murder, presumably linked to her public shaming on the Web.

* * *

Have you ever skimmed through a Big Tech corporation's mission statement (the company document that, on paper, summarises that business's very reason for being)? I do it relatively often, since I find it provides useful indications on the image that tech firms want to project to the outside world. This is why I'm going to look more closely at the mission of the platforms implicated in Tiziana's story (and in countless other digital violence cases). I promise you'll be interested in what I found.

According to a recent statement of objectives, Facebook aspires to 'bring the world closer together'. YouTube's is all about their mission to 'give everyone a voice and show them the world'. As for Twitter (less involved in Tiziana's story but, as we've seen, one of the most toxic online spaces globally), its mission is to 'give everyone the power to create and share ideas and information instantly, without barriers.' Google, on the other hand, says its purpose is to 'organise the world's information and make it universally accessible and useful.'

It turns out these mission statements are very important to our analysis. Social media companies use them heavily to defend themselves when someone accuses them of not doing enough to protect women's safety, or human rights and democracy. The version of the story their statements seek to convey is that big platforms are designed to connect people and enable the exchange of ideas and information. So how can they, despite all their good intentions, avoid giving a platform to the bigotry and violence already present in our societies? Or, to put it bluntly: if misogynists (or racists, or homophobes, or abuse perpetrators) use Google's or Facebook's extraordinary technologies to express their views and perpetrate their crimes, why should we blame the mere intermediaries?

As discussed already, social media companies also say they are working very hard to solve the problem. They have adopted new internal codes of conduct and have intensified their online moderation programmes (with the effects I have already examined when talking of moderators' worker rights). Even Google – a platform that is rarely mentioned in public debates on digital violence – has recently been forced to take action. Over the last few years, the search engine has received numerous removal requests from victims of non-consensual pornography (e.g. women who discovered that the explicit images extorted from them were among the first results coming up when someone googled their names). Under the pressure of recent legislation (above all, the right-to-be-forgotten protection within EU jurisprudence), the Californian corporation has had to come up with concerned PR statements and amendments to its own internal regulations.[3]

Between you and me, whatever narrative tech firms' press offices might be spinning at the moment, most of these commitments remain gestures of goodwill, generally with scarce legal value. Companies' codes of conduct, for instance, are largely internal

---

3   A few years ago, Google introduced a mechanism allowing users to signal non-consensual contents to be de-indexed. However, several digital violence survivors, feminist activists and lawyers have described the system as arbitrary and ineffective.

documents, while, for almost a decade, the entire sector has mightily opposed regulatory interventions that may make platforms more accountable. Businesses with enough funds to invest in large-scale moderation (above all, Facebook/Meta) have over time partially softened their position on regulation; all in all, however, social media companies tend to present a united front on this point. In essence, what they claim is that the volume of the content posted daily on the Web is simply too colossal for their moderation efforts to be infallible. And, after all, isn't this a reasonable and almost unavoidable price to pay, given that their technologies have provided us with an unprecedented incarnation of liberal democracy, where everything is accessible and everybody has a voice?

As you might have guessed, I have a problem or two with this way of framing the question. Therefore, to bust a few of the captious arguments put forward by Big Tech, I suggest we look, instead, at what social media platforms are very careful *not* to tell us.

* * *

Contrary to their version of the story, social media platforms do not directly connect us with other people or sources of information, as might a phone book, or, say, a community club or an encyclopedia. Platforms connect us, first and foremost, with a machine. A machine that has its own goals, is centred on a specific business model and plays a central role in stories like Tiziana Cantone's.

To understand this, let us consider a random social media user from 2015–16, who accessed some of the content disparaging my fellow Neapolitan. Let us follow him, step by step, down the black hole he got sucked into, dragging an innocent young woman right behind.

Brief but necessary note: the revenues of firms like Facebook/ Meta, YouTube and Twitter stem largely from their use of our personal data, which they extract every time we watch a video, retweet an article or like a post (a mechanism I have already explored when discussing Pornhub). This information is then elaborated to formulate nuanced predictions of our behaviours and is later passed on to clients who purchase advertisement spaces on the platforms themselves. So, a business advertising on Facebook will get a heads-up on the time and day of the week when we are more likely to pay attention to ads, or on whether we are or are not the most suitable audience for their products and services. Just like porn tubes, in a nutshell, mainstream social media also attempts to keep us hooked on their sites for as long as they can, in order to satisfy their insatiable appetite for our data. They, too, achieve this objective by resorting to various expedients, the first of which is the algorithmic manipulation of our newsfeeds.

The funding model of a corporation like Alphabet (the business conglomerate including Google and several subsidiaries) is slightly more complicated. That being said, search engines also harvest data from our online searches, as well as indirectly from everything we view and upload, and analyse and use them, among other things, to the benefit of their paying clients.

In the light of this, now let us go back to our unknown Internet user from 2015–16. For in his case, too, social media algorithms will have done their job and calculated that, considering he enjoyed updates on Tiziana, similar uploads would also be of interest. So, he would have continued to be shown content related to her story, as well as posts shared by other users who were also talking about Tiziana. In turn, the more this user viewed such posts and the more he commented on them, the more they will have also appeared on other visitors' feeds.

So far, as you might have noticed, we are still within the realm of the algorithmic cycle I started unpacking when looking at Pornhub, except the cycle by no means ends here.

Even though we still lack transparent information on the functioning of each individual social media algorithm (another worrying aspect of these platforms' conduct), it is well known that individual preferences are not the only criterion filtering what we see on our screens. It has recently been revealed that regardless of our inclinations, Facebook presents us with a series of posts classified as 'divisive', which are likely to stimulate intense emotions and keep us online to generate data. What's more divisive and more likely to keep an entire country glued to their keyboards than a story such as Tiziana Cantone's?

So much for the portrayal of social media as a neutral, blameless mirror of the worst instincts already lurking in the darkest corners of society. The machine with which we interact selects those instincts, multiplies them a hundredfold and then fans the flames.

We are aware of this Facebook/Meta policy largely because of one of the corporation's former employees, Frances Haugen, whose misadventures deserve a brief digression. Just like the other female employees we met in Chapter 2, Frances had also stopped feeling at ease in her workplace. Gradually losing faith in her employer's willingness to address problems as serious as online violence, algorithmic distortion and the political misuse of technology, she has since become one of the most famous whistle-blowers in the tech industry's entire history. And it is genuinely hard to dismiss her exposé, especially when you start intersecting it with cases like Tiziana Cantone's.

Hired as product manager of an operational unit called the Civic Integrity team, Frances was supposed to verify that Facebook made an actual positive contribution to society. Most of all, she and her colleagues monitored the spreading of misinformation and hate speech on the platform, and suggested strategies to counteract their proliferation. Yet – as Frances herself told the press, with which she shared hundreds of private company documents – the team's activities constantly clashed with the corporation's commercial objectives. According to the engineer-turned-conscientiousness objector, the Civic Integrity team did its best to alert Facebook's leadership to the worst risks, but their warnings constantly went unheeded, until the unit's dismantlement after the 2020 US presidential elections. Perhaps unsurprisingly, Meta executives strenuously rejected her accusations, maintaining that members of her team had been simply integrated into other divisions, and portraying Frances's disclosures as biased and excessive. Yet not even Mark Zuckerberg has been able to convincingly prove her wrong.

In the light of this account, Facebook's behaviour following Tiziana Cantone's death appears hypocritical and rather crass. Read the statements the company made in the aftermath of the tragedy. While expressing sympathy, they protested that, after all, the then notorious videos 'had never been circulated on Facebook in their entirety'. This very same argument was even used to (unsuccessfully) appeal against the Neapolitan judges' verdict. Not a single word was said about the way Facebook's algorithm contributed to making

Tiziana's story go viral and condemned her to over a year of persecution.

Since the very beginning, however, I have been saying that the focal point of the discussion should not be the conduct of any single firm, but the wider technological, economic and social structure in which these companies are enmeshed, and the perversity of the relationships between the different actors that constitute it. Tiziana's story truly is a textbook case.

For a start, Tiziana's notoriety on social media prompted a domino effect that spread all over the Web. It dramatically increased the popularity of the young woman's sex videos on adult websites, including tubes such as Pornhub. While thousands of Internet users frantically searched for Tiziana's videos (or devoured updates about her on social media and the online press), search engines such as Google liberally fed on this new indexable content and on the data that could be extracted from all that typing. A real godsend to the algorithms' owners, but a thorn in Tiziana's side, given that her name became inextricably tied to slanderous content.

To be honest, this is precisely why the part of the Neapolitan judges' ruling that relieves Google of any responsibility towards Tiziana has always left me very perplexed. I won't delve into the verdict's details (although I will return to the legal side of digital violence in Part 3), but I will ask you to remember that, far from simply cataloguing what is on the Web, whenever it has suited its purposes Google has effectively manipulated its search results. (For example, it has done so to give visibility to the advertisements of its paying clients, or to respect the censorship policies imposed by countries such as China.) So we may perhaps ask ourselves: *Shouldn't the same treatment be granted to non-consensual pornography victims who beg to get their images de-indexed?* Or is their plight to be considered less important than Google's own commercial goals?

Last but not least, there's the issue of the intricate interactions between social networks and the mainstream media: another turning point in Tiziana's saga. Just consider that, in my native Italy, over 30 per cent of the adult population get their news from Facebook, while 4.5 million people use social networks as their only source of information. Italian figures are hardly exceptional: in the UK in 2019 nearly half of the country's adults got their information from social media.

Just try to consider the effects of this actual revolution in our way of understanding the world on the traditional mainstream press, which, even before the advent of social media, has long been struggling to compete with the endless flux of information freely available online. Not that seen in this light Italian newspapers' behaviour towards Tiziana feels more justifiable, but doesn't it seem so much more understandable? In fact, it only takes a look at the headlines and writing style of many international news sites to notice that social media has become for many journalists not only a source of news stories, but also a vehicle to attract and engage readers. Which is why a story like Tiziana's, born out of the Web and still on everyone's lips after months of digital harassment, could be expected to attract clicks and views – the holy grail of a large part of the online press.

It goes without saying that profiteering is never admissible. If a big news site throws itself like a vulture on a random Internet story and even publishes the names of the protagonists it can do much to enhance its visibility and weight (something that several

Italian reporters were forced to admit, apologising for their role in Tiziana's demise).

So let us also name names. Let us say loud and clear that Tiziana and countless others did not suffer at the hands of a mysterious, headless, uncontrollable entity called 'the Internet'. They were, instead, sacrificed on the altar of a circular economy, where attention generated by the press makes for addictive feeds on social media and traffic on porn channels, and vice versa. And let us acknowledge equally plainly that until this mechanism is dismantled digital platforms' justifications will be nothing but chatter and marketing.

* * *

As a university researcher, I have devoted a great part of the last five years to studying the various manifestations of online violence to which women like Tiziana Cantone, Jess Phillips, Carolina Picchio and Rose Kalemba have been subjected. As a feminist activist, I have also participated in, and sometimes led, awareness-raising campaigns, training for schools and universities, and workshops for policy-makers and the media across the UK, Italy and the EU bubble. In so doing, over time I have been pleased to observe a remarkable improvement in the public understanding of the phenomenon. Countries from all continents have begun to introduce legislation addressing different types of digital abuse, including non-consensual pornography and teenage cyberbullying. (In Italy, legal reforms have taken place thanks to the untiring efforts of Tiziana Cantone's mother and Carolina Picchio's father.) Both nationally and internationally, charities and foundations, many guided by online violence survivors or their loved ones, are working to promote a conscious use of social media, especially among the younger generations. And the United Nations and other international agencies are also pressuring tech companies to tackle the problem.

Another positive step I have observed is an increased sensitivity not only to online violence, but also to its gender dimension. Gradually but steadily, authoritative studies have convinced a vast majority that women (particularly certain demographics of women) are differently and more intensely exposed to digital attacks. At the same time, in the wake of tragedies like Tiziana's and Carolina's, it has become harder to argue that 'online trolling doesn't kill you'. As it is now harder to deny that the Internet has provided new tools to police women's behaviours (for instance, by publicly shaming them for having had sex on camera, or for having drunk too much vodka at a party). Furthermore, a few technical solutions appear to be emerging as I write, in the form of software capable of recognising intimate images previously signalled by non-consensual pornography survivors even without the intervention of human moderators.

This progress makes me hopeful and I believe it should be acknowledged and celebrated, because it is only through building a stronger awareness of what's happening that we will be able to find effective solutions. But I wouldn't be entirely honest if I didn't add that in the public debate on online violence I continue to notice an elephant in the room. And the elephant is the economic side of all that abuse.

Mind you, I am by no means suggesting that no one else has so far recognised the role of social media companies in facilitating the online assault on women. What I am saying, though, is that in too many cases the conversation remains framed in terms that are advantageous to them. Most of all, plenty of discussions in parliaments and in the press still focus on the types of content that should or should not be allowed on the Web. (*Should we allow sexist insults on Twitter? And is 'dumb bit*h' sexist enough to be policed? Is a stolen bikini picture a non-consensual nude?* And so on and so forth.) This focus, however, has various enormous limitations.

First of all, it allows big platforms to preserve the narrative that presents them as innocent intermediaries, merely mirroring the violence and prejudice already rampant in the 'outside world'. Secondly, it ignores the links between social media and other economic actors profiting from women's suffering (porn tubes, search engines, irresponsible media, down to other online services such as private chatlines). And thirdly, this narrow interpretation erases the very heart of the problem: namely, the way many social media algorithms and digital business models select and encourage gendered abusive interactions.

If ever there was a need to repeat it, neither am I arguing that sexism, misogyny and gender-based violence have been invented by social media. That would be an absurd simplification, from which I have tried hard to stay away. Still, it would be equally absurd (and equally damaging) to ignore how digital platforms' monetisation strategies are enabling gross violations of women's fundamental right to exert control over their intimacy, their bodies and what of themselves they choose to share with others.

I refer you to Part 3 for some ideas on how to stop this mechanism. For the time being, though, I'll let you ponder one last fact. By acting as they do, the leaders of today's digital economy have instilled new life into a characteristic tendency of the great capitalist and patriarchal machine. That tendency is to slowly but inexorably transform every aspect of human life into an economic resource.

And nowadays, what is being converted into cash is our most private and intimate information, in the form of user data. And the fatter the capitalist and patriarchal machine gets, the more it gobbles up, chews and spits out the many Tizianas of this world.

CHAPTER 5

The labour behind the clicks

One night in December 2021, dozens of women gathered outside the gates of an office block in Ghaziabad, in the Indian state of Uttar Pradesh. It was cold, and the women were wrapped with coats, blankets, scarves and hats over their saris. At regular intervals, they clapped their hands and chanted slogans against a start-up named Urban Company, whose premises were in the building beyond the gates.

Launched in 2014, Urban Company proudly calls itself 'the largest online home services platform in Asia' and operates in over 50 cities in India, Australia, Singapore, the United Arab Emirates and Saudi Arabia. Using a software technology not unlike Uber and Lyft, it connects a wide range of clients with an even wider variety of service providers: from cooks to beauticians, massage therapists to plumbers. And, as you may perhaps imagine, the gender composition of this workforce changes notably depending on the service.

It is no coincidence, for instance, that the women who rallied on that December night were all beauticians. One of them, 35-year-old Seema Singh, had a daughter who was turning four that day. 'It was my daughter's birthday as I sat there in the cold protesting against the company's unfair practices. I wanted to be with her that day,' she told the press the morning after the protest. Yet she also explained she had had no other choice.

A few months before, Seema had started to meet in public parks with a few colleagues – a term Urban Company might find inappropriate, since rather than treating the service providers registered on its platform as staff with individual and collective rights, it prefers to call them 'independent partners', deserving of 'power and autonomy'. Except the recent measures adopted by the company tell a rather different story.

To start with, there is no cap on the commission Urban Company retains on each transaction. Beginning in 2020, beauticians like Seema had begun to notice a visible increase in the fee the platform automatically cut from their earnings. More or less at the same time, the firm had also started to charge a penalty for cancelled appointments, and to pressure beauticians to receive positive reviews from their customers.

In October 2021, Seema and more than 100 of her co-workers convened outside the company offices, giving rise to the first women gig workers' strike in Indian history. Supported by an emerging gig worker union, they demanded decent earnings, a transparent mechanism to handle complaints and more attention to their safety. Their demonstration made a lot of noise and Urban Company initially seemed willing to consider their requests.

Shortly after, however, a new online booking system appears to have been imposed upon the workers, which automatically assigned less remunerative shifts to those who received lower ratings. And there was an unpleasant surprise in store even for the beauticians who obtained enthusiastic reviews: inserted into a 'plus' category, they were obliged to offer the clients a 'top experience', including compulsory discounts.

It has been reported, moreover, that the platform forced service providers to pay a substantial advance at the beginning of each month, in exchange for future 'guaranteed income': those who refused would have only been able to work a few days per week.

Feeling they had their backs against the wall, Seema and others returned to protest. But when they showed up again at Urban Company's premises, they were presented with a legal notice to appear in court. The firm called their demonstration 'illegal' and intimated that they should desist from other protests. To be precise, the court's document accused Seema and other organisers of sabotaging the relationship between the firm and its 'partners', and instigating other women to commit violence.

Seema did not let herself be bullied and refused to back off, replying that her fellow strikers were all adult women, perfectly able to make autonomous choices. 'It is wrong of Urban Company to infantilise them by saying I instigated them. They are all fully aware of their concerns with the organisation,' she said to the press a few days after.

Seema and the other women continued to protest for the entire night. A few of them were pregnant and it has been reported that Urban Company did not allow them to use the company's toilet.

* * *

Congolese miners, Chinese workers, engineers and social media moderators from all over the world are not the only women workers who make up the digital economy production cycle. Nor are they the only ones to be exploited or discriminated against. Behind all the products and services that are only a couple of clicks away, new forms of labour are hidden, and they are usually barely regulated and even less protected.

In 2020, just to give you some context, India had about 15 million gig workers, mostly employed by platforms specialising in care and home services (Urban Company being one of them) as well as food delivery (for example, Zomato and Swiggy). In England and Wales, about 4.4 million are currently offering their services through a platform at least once a week. And the global turnover is substantial. In 2019, a study from Mastercard estimated that the gig economy (also known, incidentally, as the 'platform economy') generated circa $200 billion globally. Several other reports foresee a further expansion in years to come.

The term 'gig' is, of course, quite vague, and applies to different jobs and work relationships. Some platforms mediate the supply and demand of online labour (think data insertion and analysis, content production, software development and so on). So-called 'on-demand' platforms, instead, facilitate the allocation of manual work: home services, personal care, transport, etc. But all these various sectors have at least one trait in common: the impact of the gender dimension upon workers' experiences.

Let me start by saying that the rigid gender segregation that still characterises many occupational areas is also evident within the platform economy. And the consequences aren't pretty. Where there is a minority of women operating in male-dominated gig markets – think of female drivers and riders – they face both pay discrimination and employment conditions that ignore their specific needs.

Over the last few years, for example, hundreds of female Uber drivers (as I've already mentioned) were molested by male passengers and the company has been unable to find a solution to this. Part of the problem lies in the fact that most lucrative fares on driving apps tend to be at night, which puts women drivers in a very difficult position. Some decide to drive at night while struggling with the fear of being attacked. Others prefer not to, and in countries like Australia and the USA this has contributed to a large gender pay gap among gig drivers.

Another much talked about category of gig workers is that of riders working for delivery apps, whom we have all seen a lot of since the start of the Covid-19 pandemic. Much less spoken about, however, are the specific gender injustices women riders are subjected to. This is why, in various parts of the world, they are busy protesting to defend rights that, in the twenty-first century, it is hard to believe might be denied to any worker, for example, the right to access toilet facilities.

'There are no facilities for us as workers, I have never even asked the restaurants (out of fear). I mostly just rely on petrol pumps [*sic*] in whichever areas I can find,' says Anita (pseudonym), a rider from Mumbai who delivers meals for the Zomato app. And – as emphasised by many gig trade unionists – women have once more the worst side of the bargain, since many of them do not feel able to urinate in public. According to Rinku Sharma, who worked for a platform called Ola and the vice president of an emerging union of Indian app-based transport workers, 'Many women try to hold their pee in. It goes up to 10–12 hours sometimes as well.' Rinku also adds that, 'If a woman has had an operation or a Caesarean, they can't hold in for so long and they face bodily difficulties.' As a consequence, some female drivers carry around bottles full of urine for the entire day, while others abstain from drinking for as many hours as possible.

If I shift my attention away from riders and drivers and move, instead, to highly feminised sections of the gig economy, things do not appear to change much. A paradigmatic example is cleaning apps. These are increasingly popular applications whereby you can book a one-off clean of your house or office. As you have probably guessed, it is mainly women who offer their services through these platforms (suffice to say that one of the most famous is called MaidsApp). And, equally predictably, they have been asking for better protection; above all they've asked to receive further information on the houses they are sent to clean. Just try to imagine how they might feel – travelling from one location to another, cleaning products in hand, with the prospect of reaching an unknown, perhaps isolated house, with no idea who'll open the door.

Some women may choose to say no to a gig not due to fear, but to the very low earnings they can make out of most apps. 'I won't take any job that costs more than 20 rand [about $1.38] to get to. It's nice to get work, but I don't want to spend it all on travel,' says a South African woman named Nomagugu Sibanda to non-profit Rest of World. She works as a nanny and housekeeper through the app SmartMaid. 'When I get a booking, I look at the map carefully to see where it is before accepting a request.'

There are situations in which gender and class inequalities intersect with disparities based on age, race and cultural identity, for example in both South Asia and North America, and specifically in the care sector. In both regions, the booming of home services apps has made life difficult for older women and for those without Internet access, who might feel ill at ease with a smartphone or be unable to connect to Wi-Fi. Gig care workers belonging to ethnic minorities within their respective countries have it particularly hard for different reasons. To begin with, many apps force them to keep up-to-date profiles complete with pictures and personal details, not unlike those on social networks. Apart from costing them time and energy, this contributes to a stereotyped narrative where African American and Latina women, or those belonging to a given Indian caste, are the ones expected to take on the burden of house chores and other care-related activities. Plus, precisely because care work has historically been performed by women (and by women with a certain demographic profile), it also tends to be belittled and poorly paid. Not only are care platforms careful not to correct this trend, with their photo galleries and cheesy online marketing they also subliminally reinforce existing racist and sexist associations.

Not even women who offer remote professional services, such as online editing and counselling, are safe from exploitation and inequalities. I'd like to mention one sector in particular: the controversial online therapy industry, pioneered by companies such as BetterHelp and Talkspace. 'I choose not to be part of [Talkspace] because they pay therapists too little,' said Katie Ziskind, a licensed marriage and family therapist, to *Salon* magazine. She had gone through the application process in 2018. 'These programs actually devalue the rate and the worth of a therapist because they paid so little per hour.'

Now, there is no doubt that a mental health professional is

relatively privileged when compared to a driver or a rider. But it is also true that women like Katie are still faced with some of the most typical disadvantages of platform work, such as the lack of paid holidays and maternity leave. Moreover, apart from being offered trifling earnings, they are painfully aware of both the scarce protections offered to online therapy clients and of the impossibility to interact with co-workers and organise together for better pay and conditions.

And here's, truly, what lies at the heart of the matter. The public discourse on the gig economy, made to measure to meet the needs of gig platforms, puts at the centre words such as 'flexibility', 'autonomy', even 'female empowerment' and 'work–life balance'. Over the last decade, this encouraged many women to offer their services through these apps. It's just that the flexibility ended up giving rise to a toxic combination of endless shifts, extreme economic uncertainty and insufficient protections.

Whether a woman offers online face massage courses, house cleaning or video and audio editing, her status as a 'contractor' or 'partner' (or whatever definition a company may come up with not to call her 'employee') deprives her of historically acquired rights and any means of collective negotiation. So much, then, for all the talk of flexibility. Free from many standard obligations of an employer, the platform she works for can force her hand by penalising her for choosing to make herself available only on certain days or time slots, or for taking longer breaks.

And gig companies have devised even subtler strategies to make profit from their workers: for instance, by obliging them to purchase in advance make-up or cleaning products to use when providing their services. Even more problematic, however, is that the intertwining of gig work and technology allows companies to individualise and divide the workforce, undermining the protests of those who dare to speak up and demonising activists like Seema Singh, as though they were saboteurs and instigators.

Have a little think the next time you feel like thanking Uber or Deliveroo for having made your life easier. And think, above all, of the forces that are hidden behind the car that arrives or the ready-to-eat dinner you get delivered with one click.

* * *

Drivers, riders and other gig workers are not the only ones who are bogged down in the new frontiers of oppression opened by digital capitalism and some of the most vulnerable worker categories are not necessarily the most obvious ones. If I say 'influencer', I'm sure you'll think of the Kardashian sisters, or of other celebrities who, across the world, seem to live luxurious existences, filled with holidays, gourmet dining and designer clothes subsidised by brands eager to capitalise from their social media posts. But not all influencers are in this category; their reality is rather different.

Nellie, an African American blogger and influencer, lives in New York City and blogs on parenting, food and fitness under the pseudonym Brooklyn Active Mama. 'You have to be prepared to get paid at any time. It's very difficult for an influencer; if you sign a $2,000 contract, you really never know when you're going to get that money,' she said to *The Atlantic* magazine. She added that after having worked for a Pepsi social media campaign – a job she had got through Speakr (a website which puts brands in touch with content creators) – she had to wait eight months to receive the agreed upon

$200 payment. There are many Nellies in the world of influencer marketing.

For a start, it is important to know that we are talking about a flourishing, sizeable market, which is expected to exceed $15 billion shortly. It is a market that includes, apart from intermediaries like Speakr (which several influencers have reported to the press to notably delay digital creatives' payments), a plethora of brands (of the calibre of Disney, Sony and Microsoft, all known to commission influencer campaigns) and social media platforms hosting sponsored content. Here's another crucial piece of information: this varied industry relies largely on female labour. Consider, for instance, that according to data analysis firm Statista, out of about 3 million posts published in 2019 by influencers on Instagram, more than 80 per cent were created by women.

This sector, however, is organised as a pyramid. On the top there is a small group of stars, whose posts are viewed by millions and provide them with a more or less safe income. Down the influencer hierarchy, we find a crowd of micro-, nano- and aspiring influencers, who aim to reach a specific niche of Web users and invest hours of unpaid work to gather social media contacts so as to secure their first commissions. Early on in their careers, it is not rare for influencers to work for free or for very little compensation in the hope of 'getting themselves out there'. It's also not unusual, when a brand or a platform like Speakr postpones their payment yet again, for influencers to hesitate to complain or cut contact, mostly because those commissions enable them to pay their bills and they can't afford to gain a reputation as being someone who is 'difficult to work with'.

As always, these discriminations and injustices are stratified.

Stephanie Yeboah, a Black and plus-size influencer and author based in London, has been blogging and posting for years on matters of gender, race and body image. She has won awards and been invited to speak about her work at festivals and conferences. Yet in 2015 she found out that white influencers contributing to the same campaign as her got paid more, even though she had more followers and a higher engagement rate on her content. And not having, at the time, an agent, or a trade union to support her, she didn't dare protest to the company that had hired her for the campaign.

More recently, following George Floyd's murder in 2020 and the explosion of the Black Lives Matter movement, many companies anxious to 'diversify' their digital marketing have contacted Black women who create sponsored videos on Instagram and TikTok. Recently published research, however, shows that Black, lesbian, transgender, disabled and plus-size female influencers remain underpaid on most platforms. Some African American dancers and artists, in particular, decided to strike against TikTok in 2021 after discovering that their performances were often appropriated and copied by white TikTokers, preventing them from monetising those activities.

For these and all the reasons so far summarised, influencers and online content producers have begun to mobilise collectively on both sides of the Atlantic. In the UK, the Creator Union has recently emerged: the first national union of Internet creatives, tellingly launched by two women, mixed-race blogger Nicole Ocran and digital marketer Kat Molesworth. In the US, another woman, Qianna Smith Bruneteau, has founded the non-profit American Influencer Council. Both organisations fight to ensure more transparency and fairer employment conditions for digital creators. Both build on the idea that unity is strength, which is crucial in this kind of freelance work, just like the myriad of other professions within the platform economy, an economy that favours workers' isolation and often a very competitive work environment. These organisations recognise two fundamental truths: first, that people who do the same job tend to have common interests; and second, that such interests should be protected and recognised. It is not by chance that in many parts of the world these emerging unions are developing alongside other forms of collective organising, including class actions initiated by digital creators. Some of you will have heard of Bria Kam and Chrissy Chambers. They are, perhaps, the most famous lesbian couple on YouTube of all time. Together with other LGBTQ+ video-makers, Bria and Chrissy sued YouTube in 2019, accusing the platform of classifying as 'adult content' (making it harder to monetise) an LGBTQ+ themed video, which contained no nudity and violated no platform guidelines. At the time of publication this case is ongoing.

I personally find it very significant (and, in all honesty, quite outrageous) that such courageous initiatives are often ridiculed and belittled as 'rebellions of the Web's pretty girls'. For even beyond the undeniable sexism permeating these comments, they also betray the desire to undermine the political value of influencers organising. It seems to me that it is in the interest of many to portray digital women workers as lazy and spoiled little girls, who should be grateful to have such a 'cool' way to make ends meet. In doing so, a layer of condescending glamour is kept over the misunderstood world of influencing, and those who make a living out of producing online content are infantilised and patronised. Since every worker deserves rights and safety, we could start by affording these women the minimal level of respect and take them seriously.

* * *

Perhaps you do not pay your bills doing deliveries for an app or posting videos online; however, the role of platform worker applies to a certain extent to each and every one of us – with an overwhelming majority being by no means compensated for their labour.

I first started reflecting on this a few years ago, during a seminar at the beginning of my PhD. At that time in our lives, my colleagues and I were all scared to death of: a) not being able to finish our dissertation; b) not publishing well enough to gain an academic post after graduating; and c) even with the best publications and theses in the world, not surviving, let alone thriving, in a saturated and precarious academic job market. The man giving the seminar, however, clearly thought all these concerns were not enough and he made sure to add to our list of worries. According to him, no one would give us a university job if we did not tweet as much as possible about our research, post pictures of our talks and conferences on LinkedIn and keep an up-to-date page on platforms like Academia.edu and ResearchGate. As you know, any prospective employer these days won't invite you for an interview without googling you first.

Several years have passed and I have noticed that these pressures do not necessarily reduce as you progress in your career: a (female) colleague of mine, who is ten years older than me and is considered an authority in her discipline, was recently told she should 'make herself more visible online'.

On the one hand, these trends are better understood as part of a wider context: that of the ongoing commercialisation of university research and, more generally, of the increasing *brandisation* of our lives. And both tendencies have been intensified by the digital revolution.

On the other hand, however, seminar after seminar, and subliminal message after subliminal message (*Digitise your lectures and upload them on YouTube! Write yet another blog, needless to say, for free! And don't forget to share it on social media!*) a few questions come to mind. To be specific, I have mostly started to ask myself questions about how platforms take advantage of this situation. And I am not the only one who has been busy thinking.

Several critical economists have been studying the dynamic I just described and have given it a name: *prosumption*, a hybrid of production and consumption. The idea behind the concept is that platform capitalism thrives not only thanks to the more or less underpaid labour of those who offer online services or create online content but it is also kept alive by millions of Internet users, who, independently from our professions, post updates on apps and sites, make our data available and give the Web economic value, without being remunerated at all.

Major platforms, as we have seen, may differ substantially in their business models, but, without exception, they all push us to stay constantly connected, completely digitising ourselves and our personal and professional interactions, which they will turn into money.

What is perhaps less known and less studied is the role that gender plays in all this. I am not denying that men are also trapped in the prosumption cycle, but many platforms deliberately and openly target female audiences. Think of Pinterest, think of Instagram (to which I will return later on). Think of how on many professional digital platforms, women are pushed to share more personal updates than those published by their male colleagues. And think of how, according to many testimonies, that is barely their choice. In many industries, women are under-represented, underpaid and comparatively less visible, which drives them to be particularly present online. To this, we must add that many organisations encourage their female employees to develop a 'personal brand' and to 'speak up online', hoping to appear as egalitarian and 'women-friendly' workplaces.

Obviously, nobody can deny this unprecedented type of exploitation is often carried out with our more or less conscious collaboration. In other words, many of us derive some advantages from participating in the prosumption mechanism: from personal gratification to professional benefits.

Amid contradictions and ambiguities, I am no exception. Albeit seeking to limit the time I spend online, I continue to this day to use various platforms to present my studies outside academia, or to promote feminist initiatives and campaigns. I do this because I feel that the minimum we can do is to interact critically with the digital world, but it is also impossible and counterproductive to give up all online engagement. Or at least this is the conclusion I reach when I think about it more logically. No matter how long I have studied the way social media work and the impact they have on people's well-being, there are times when I still let myself be engrossed by them.

Plus, in my case as in that of millions of others, there is another relevant part of the story: namely, the complex intersections between online activism, platforms and social movements.

Like it or not, these days political activism (including feminism) is also built and spread online. Yet here, too, we are drowning in a sea of contradictions. I confess that I have yet to meet an activist who feels she can completely escape some form of self-exploitation when using social media and digital platforms in general. 'I am addicted to social networks,' said a friend of mine to me recently; a sister-in-arms who devotes her time and energy to the fight for LGBTQ+ and disabled people's rights. 'I get anxious whenever a post I did for a campaign does not get enough likes. And I spend hours reading other relevant updates, without even noticing. And then, as regular as one can be, I go and post again on one platform or another.' Many of us, at least from time to time, have come to recognise ourselves in these words. And digital platforms, as we know, are ready to cash in.

Among those studying digital capitalism, metaphors abound that try to capture the role that we as platform users play within the digital economy. Are we all platform workers (unpaid and, to a great extent, exploited)? Are we a mere product, sold by tech companies to advertisers and paying customers? Or are we, to cite Professor Shoshana Zuboff of Harvard University, 'carcasses' that platforms throw away after having extracted from us the value they are after? Each of these has its merits and the debate is still open. As far as I am concerned, I think that, depending on the case, we may be playing all these different roles. But I would also specify that it is women that digital capitalism exploits more methodically and more ruthlessly.

* * *

What's work, and what's not work? This question is at least a few centuries older than the digital revolution. And it has inspired countless rebellions, many of which were led by women. Starting from the aftermath of the Second World War, feminist activists and researchers, like Silvia Federici, guided struggles in several countries for the recognition of housework as work. More recently, considerably more attention has been paid to 'emotional labour': the cluster of historically feminine (and therefore historically undervalued) activities that psychologically support people and communities. It is interesting to notice the similarities in this 'social reproduction' labour and the new forms of work enabled by the platform economy. Another well-known academic, Kylie Jarrett, has been writing for a while of those who consume and produce unpaid online content as 'digital housewives', offering a gender perspective on the problem. 'Post-workerist' scholars such as Tiziana Terranova have also been reflecting on the ideas of 'cognitive' and 'immaterial' labour taking place online, and on its gender dimension.

These discussions are anything but sterile or intellectual disputes. The point is that from the moment we recognise a given activity as work then, at least on paper, a series of legal and political protections should come into place. But within digital capitalism, the definitions of 'work' and 'worker' have become so blurred that many an economic operator turns this to their advantage, to the detriment of human and women's rights.

In Chapter 2, I examined how digital capitalism is maintained by a long series of women workers, all oppressed, due to their gender and at times intersectional identities, even more intensely than their male colleagues. Aside from these categories, we now know we should also include gig workers, influencers and digital creators. And, with all respect to the differences, we should include ourselves. We, the Internet users, who update our LinkedIn profile late at night because our boss asked us to. We, the feminist activists, who get discouraged when the post promoting an initiative we have been slaving away for weeks on obtains few views on Facebook, only to find out that the platform has now altered its algorithms, so that the circulation of posts from 'social' and 'political' pages gets automatically reduced anyway. We, who hope to succeed in the impossible, titanic enterprise of defeating the machine, and post again and again, ultimately finding ourselves enveloped in the tight, gendered Web of the Internet's circular economy machine.

However, the image of the woman as a defenceless victim is a trope I try hard to stay away from (even when reporting stories of unspeakable violence). Nor is it my intention to present any of us as powerless beings; this is not just out of political belief, but also for truth's sake. For the evidence is out there for all to see: women digital creatives, gig workers, social media moderators and all the other female digital labourers are organising for their rights. And if digital patriarchal capitalism is there to devour us and engulf us, we refuse to play its game, or at least to play it within conditions we haven't chosen. Those who wish to join the resistance are free to do so (and to go and check out Part 3, where I'll talk about how to resist).

CHAPTER 6

The women's pandemic

My friend Elisa belongs to a category of people I never ceased to admire during the Covid-19 pandemic: working mums faced with closed nurseries and toddlers crawling all over the house.

Elisa and her husband do the same job and during lockdown they both worked remotely from the British city where they live. When she showed up on a video call with her son on her lap, no one batted an eyelid. A colleague said jokingly: 'Oh, how adorable, we have got a mascot in the call today.' However, when her husband did the same thing, his boss told him that 'you can't work with a child in your arms' and that 'you could always take some unpaid leave'. Since him taking unpaid leave would have notably affected the family budget, Elisa ended up minding her child for most of the lockdown.

Another friend of mine, Zoë, is a playwright by training (but once the virus paralysed the theatre industry, she also started to teach English in a school). She has got one undergraduate and two master's degrees, and is very resourceful. She has crossed half of South East Asia by bike, and another time she survived a night on the Rocky Mountains with a bear trying to enter her tent. During the pandemic, she realised that the time she was spending on social media didn't help her feel at ease with the woman she is: intelligent and courageous. On the contrary, it lowered her self-esteem, and triggered her anxieties and insecurities.

'On Twitter I kept on visualising updates from those few playwrights who could still find work, while I was at home, watching my entire sector collapse and feeling powerless,' she told me on a summer afternoon in 2020, when we were finally allowed to walk together in the park. 'Instagram, instead, would just show to me pictures of fashionistas and gym pros with perfect bodies, who seemed to spend the lockdown exercising and trying on new outfits. Initially I found it hard to keep away. Then I made a good decision and deleted most of my accounts.'

I know plenty of stories like Elisa's and Zoë's, since there are lots of smart women in my life and many of them have a complicated relationship with technology, which became even more complex due to Covid-19. For example, I could tell you about my various single friends who, between lockdowns, relied even more than usual on dating apps such as Tinder and Bumble, given the impossibility of meeting new people in person. After that, though, they stayed away for several weeks: they had had enough of being insulted by users they had rejected and being sent unsolicited photos of male genitalia.

'Getting to know new people is out of the question, and since I live with flatmates, I have more than my own personal safety to think about,' one of them said to me at the beginning of 2021. 'But then, when I go on the app, I start worrying not about the risk of contagion, but about being molested.'

I could also share some of the experiences I went through during the pandemic. For instance, I could tell you of the many unwanted propositions I received online, or of the more and more frequent invitations to speak or write for free about topics on which I have professional expertise, all coming from organisations that were expecting to monetise my work. I am not referring to university lectures or activist speaking gigs (if I am free, I always say yes to these, no matter the fee). But once all live events got cancelled, plenty of media groups and professional event planners went on the hunt for experts willing to speak from their living rooms. And it's quite something to realise that an agency that argues that an even minimal speaking fee couldn't possibly be squeezed into their tight budget would charge viewers several hundreds of pounds. In one of my favourite exchanges, after I politely declined his invitation an event organiser asked me: 'Couldn't you send me a list of your free dates in the next few weeks and I will book you in for whatever event is on, no matter the topic?' On another occasion someone asked: 'I get you don't want to work for free, but do you have any friends who might?'

Alternatively, I could tell you of the time the chair of a feminist webinar I was contributing to (this time, in return for a perfectly fair fee) told me I should be careful. This was because trolls had tried to disrupt her organisation's events, appearing on camera without their underwear. This behaviour is known as 'zoom bombing' and it exploded in 2020–21, and appears to have been used particularly to disturb women-only and feminist meet-ups.

Quite evidently, the Covid-19 pandemic was both a mirror and an accelerator of pre-existing trends. At a time when, like it or not, we had to rely on the Internet more than ever to work, pursue our interests and keep in touch with our loved ones, it is no wonder that the negative sides of technology manifested themselves with even greater clarity. When in lockdown, many of us were, of course, grateful for the devices that enabled us to stay in contact with the rest of the world and, often, to carry on paying our bills. But while tech companies' profits grew even fatter thanks to us being confined in our homes in front of a screen, many technology-induced problems felt more serious than ever.

Which is why, instead of saying more about myself or the women I love, I'll provide you with a glimpse of the bigger picture.

* * *

In 2020, the *Financial Times* published a list of the world's companies that most benefitted from the pandemic. In every economic and social crisis of the capitalist age there are winners and there are losers and, apart from the pharmaceutical companies involved in vaccine production, most of the winners were in the tech industry.

Rather tellingly, in first, second and third places on the *FT* ranking were: Amazon (uncontested titan of online shopping), Microsoft (proprietor, among other things, of the work application Teams) and Apple (whose sales rose steeply as soon as people decided high-quality gadgets might be a good investment when working remotely). Just behind them are Facebook/Meta (profiting from the boom of social media interactions during lockdowns), Google/Alphabet and various other digital businesses, including the videoconference service Zoom, virtually unknown to most until spring 2020.

In line with these firms' returns, however, online sexism skyrocketed, which the entire sector hasn't yet dealt with properly.

Digital violence against women has proliferated since the earliest Covid-19 outbreaks. An escalation of gender-based Internet harassment was registered, for example, by both UN agencies and specialised NGOs in countries as diverse as Australia, Great Britain, India and in several Middle Eastern and North African areas. Many of the attacks took place on social media and were, sadly, of the sort that we have come to expect. However, new forms of assaults also boomed, with several digital businesses that boosted their profits during the pandemic still struggling to grant women a safe and egalitarian user experience.

A particularly interesting case is that of the videoconference services industry, which rapidly turned into a multimillion-dollar business thanks to the sudden, forced digitisation of our existences. Do you remember the zoom bombing warning I was given by the host of the feminist webinar? Well, you should know that during the pandemic the very same phenomenon infested school, university, work and political meetings globally. Zoom calls and other online events were invaded by trolls who disrupted them with sexist (or racist, or homophobic, or otherwise bigoted) words or images. Extreme pornography was also a popular choice. And I promise you that it's no fun, especially for young women who go online expecting to join a class (or, perhaps, a feminist book club) and are thoroughly unprepared to be targeted.

Other cyberspaces that were rife with misogyny during Covid were the comment sections of many online newspapers, as well as instant messaging services like WhatsApp and Telegram, and the galaxy of online gaming (of which we'll learn more in Chapter 7).

If only to do justice to my single friends I mentioned above, though, the one sector I really want to tell you about is the online dating industry.

Contrary to what you might think, the Covid-19 pandemic hasn't left dating applications broke. In fact, the Match Group conglomerate (which owns Tinder, OkCupid and several other dating sites) saw its income rise by almost 20 per cent in 2020. People, of course, wanted to distract themselves, so a number of apps cleverly met this need by launching video chat services and other lockdown-proof options. As online interactions have significantly increased in these spaces, so has sexual harassment.

Female users have had to put up with endless instances of 'cyber-flashing' (receiving unwanted sexual photos, generally penis pictures). A very telling detail is that this form of non-consensual pornography has also become widespread on applications like Bumble – a supposedly feminist site, where men are not permitted to contact a woman unless she has previously agreed to it. Nevertheless, Bumble itself has recently made it known that in the UK alone nearly half of its women users under the age of 24 have been subjected to cyber-flashing during the Covid pandemic. (Needless to say, male app users were significantly less exposed.) Just imagine what happens on other apps.

Online violence is not the only gendered face of digital capitalism, nor is it the only one to have manifested itself especially forcefully during the pandemic. Women worldwide have been exploited by a number of digital platforms, which, as we saw in Chapter 5, have long treated them as producers of data, attention and other precious currencies within the digital economy. And which, during the pandemic, seem to have got even worse.

Take, for instance, the effects of lockdown Instagram use on teenage girls, which was much discussed in the press in the autumn of 2021. Some of you may already know that all this attention was at least partially due to information leaked by someone we've previously encountered: Meta's brave ex-product manager-turned-whistle-blower Frances Haugen. Among other disclosures, Frances revealed that Instagram tends to redirect adolescent girls towards posts and videos that lower their self-esteem and celebrate extreme thinness and anorexia. 'From very innocuous topics like healthy recipes' – she explained to the US Congress – Instagram's algorithm leads children 'all the way to anorexia-promoting content, over a very short period of time.'

The mechanism Frances refers to is, of course, always the same, the one you should know inside out by now. One video leads to another, liking a post makes you view a few more, and the machine lures you into a spiral of increasingly toxic content, since its only objective is to generate more data and raise advertisement returns. The particular effects that this mechanism produced during Covid are epitomised by my friend Zoë's anecdote. But Zoë is an adult, who knows how to take care of her mental and physical health, while young girls' situations were naturally quite different. During the health crisis, they found themselves with even more time on their hands but with even less support available. Should it come as a surprise that they were affected by the algorithm's toxic loop even more deeply than usual?

What is worse, Meta executives were always, according to Frances Haugen, perfectly aware of this situation and they simply refused to intervene. 'The company's leadership knows ways to make Facebook and Instagram safer and won't make the necessary changes because they have put their immense profits before people,' were Frances's words in her opening statement at Washington DC's Capitol.

So, to summarise: the world's population went through a life-altering crisis that hit women and adolescent girls even harder than other groups. And now we are told that at such a difficult time one of the world's most controversial tech giants, which was plumping its revenues all along, was either unwilling, or at best unable, to protect at-risk teenage girls. I don't know about you, but I find this a rather sobering thought.

Finally, there is a last trend that emerged during the pandemic which I'd like to explore. I am sure you have not forgotten the early months of 2020, when millions of us started working from home and had to put in lots of extra hours to digitise daily tasks. Raise your hand if you have been asked to participate in endless 'emergency calls' on Zoom or to record infinite online presentations? Raise your hand, too, if you have friends or relatives who found themselves drowning in similarly time- and energy-consuming endeavours, but had to put on a brave face, because 'at least they were working, unlike the neighbour who had lost her job'?

Now stop for a moment to consider how, following school and nursery closures, many women had to combine this already augmented workload with new care obligations. Not that, obviously, care should necessarily be equated with womanhood. Yet the story of my friend Elisa is a case in point. Judging from available statistics, female smart workers from all over the world truly spent their lockdown with the laptop in one hand and the baby bottle – or the older kids' homework – in the other.

Some of the most depressing stats come from North America, where a report from management consulting firm McKinsey found that about one working mother out of three has had to scale down her career objectives during the pandemic, or has thought about quitting work – without necessarily being able to afford it. Two factors seem to have led to this. First, an increase in childcare duties during lockdown. And second, some substantial changes caused by the full digitisation of women's work and family life: think having to help kids with remote learning, always being on call when working from home since 'after all we're all in lockdown without nothing else to do, right?'

Women in the UK found themselves in the same situation. Various studies have documented how UK-based women workers took on a much larger share of unpaid caring for children. As reported by the Office for National Statistics, a significantly higher proportion of women than men had to supervise the home-schooling of their children. And, based on this, University College London researchers have noted that injustices in the division of unpaid care work have put women at higher risk of psychological distress.

So, we clearly face significant problems. As to the cause of those problems? It seems obvious to me that any man refusing to take on his share of household responsibilities and childcare has to take some blame. And huge difficulties originated from the sexist biases of bosses and line managers (women's as well as their partners'; think again of my friend Elisa's story). The bosses who said to female employees that since they were in smart work they should 'send that email after the last feed'. And who told their male employees that 'it is up to mothers to take care of children's online lessons'. While these gendered power relations were ubiquitous well before Covid and even before the digital revolution, the transition to remote work has strengthened them.

So much, then, for the idea that 'we are all in this together' and 'the entire economy is in the same boat' (the chosen mantras of governments and employers since the very beginning of the outbreak). In this boat, quite plainly, women have much less room than anyone else. And, in a cruel twist, the switch to a fully digitised life appears to be suffocating them even further.

*   *   *

As I'm piecing together a global (if fairly sketchy) puzzle, I went searching for personal stories that would help inform me. I'm going to start with a Kenyan woman I'll call Rose.

Just like my friend Zoë, Rose lost her job during the pandemic. And just like my other friend, Elisa, she also spent the time at home with her husband. In Rose's case, her job was running a stand at the local market from which she sold second-hand clothes; a stand that her husband gave away without her consent as soon as the government imposed the first lockdown. Apart from depriving her of her independence, her husband also beat her up so viciously that Rose was left unable to scream. He had been violent to her before, but having to stay at home with him, Rose felt completely at his mercy.

You might think that the fact that Rose lived in Kenya is not relevant to our discussion. After all, millions of jobs, mostly female ones, have been lost all over the world since the beginning of the health crisis. And due to forced cohabitations, incidents of domestic violence have dramatically risen at the global level. But two details in Rose's story are highly significant. First, Rose couldn't transfer her business online, yet the online selling of second-hand garments has been a popular lockdown activity. Second, digital apps and other online services are used in many countries to allow women to report abusive partners or to access information on available support. Rose was able to escape her husband's clutches only after a friend referred her to a local organisation, which helped her report him to the authorities. Until then, Rose didn't know who to contact and wasn't at all aware that domestic violence could be reported to the police.

We don't know whether Rose had a smartphone or any way to connect to the Internet since this detail is not included in her testimony, collected by Human Rights Watch. Everything in her story, though, suggests that she didn't. This should by no means come as a shock: the digital gender gap in Kenya is among the highest in the world. (The definition of 'digital gender gap' may vary slightly depending on the country and study, but it is mostly understood to be an index to capture gender inequalities in access to the Web and other digital technologies, with smartphone ownership making for a common indicator.)

So here's an important piece of information: before the pandemic, the Kenyan divide between female and male smartphone owners was 34 per cent. In 2020, it immediately went up no less than eight percentage points. Among the reasons for this, the GSMA (an international body that represents the interests of the world's mobile operators) cites the fact that during the pandemic lots of men invested in a smartphone to seek new work opportunities and keep in touch with friends and family. Women, however, were mostly denied that possibility and ended up feeling more isolated and less independent than ever.

To understand what's going on in Kenya, the GSMA warns, the high cost of electronic devices must be considered. They are unaffordable for many and regarded as even more of a luxury following the economic crisis caused by the virus. 'A phone is not a priority for me now,' said a 45-year-old woman who lives in rural Kenya to GSMA, 'other things are: children going to school, food, clothes.'

We are, in short, dealing with yet another circular problem. Families' financial difficulties and internal power dynamics make it hard for Kenyan women to access technology. Their being 'disconnected' makes them increasingly vulnerable to domestic violence and, more generally, to male authority, and risks undermining the future of the younger generations.

I talk about the younger generations with full knowledge of the facts. Kenyan girls and young women have been harmed by their lack of access to technology and the Internet perhaps even more than their adult counterparts. 'I do not have access to a computer, Internet, or a smartphone,' a 16-year-old schoolgirl from the city of Garissa told Human Rights Watch. Her classes were entirely transferred online after school closures. 'Because of this, I am very behind in physics, which, as it is, is already difficult.' And the reports published by Kenyan specialised NGOs are also filled with this type of testimony.

It is hard to measure exactly how many Kenyan female students were denied their right to study over the last two years because they lacked access to digital resources. As in many of the poorest parts of the world, the absence of the Internet and electronic devices intersects with other forms of gendered economic inequality. Many girls, for instance, apart from being unable to attend classes, were also asked to help out with house chores and the care of younger siblings. In some cases, they were even forced to marry as soon as possible to help their families cope with Covid-related financial struggles. It is obvious that until these young women have access to electronic devices and the Internet just as their male peers do, their futures will suffer because of it.

So now take the time to stop and answer this question honestly. However sympathetic you might have felt towards these Kenyan girls and women, have you perhaps been thinking that their plight is not a concern where you live? If so, I'm afraid I'll have to shatter your illusions. There is equally alarming data from all over the world, including very close to home.

* * *

I don't want to bombard you with figures, but those that follow are important to give us a true picture of what's going on.

According to the global network Alliance for Affordable Internet (A4AI), men globally are 21 per cent more likely than women to be online. This gap increases to 52 per cent in the least developed countries, but remains high in Europe and North America. Two further important details: one, digital gender disparities have remained high over the last decade; and two, during Covid their impact has hit women even harder than usual.

Based on A4AI's estimates, women's exclusion from digital technology cost the world a total loss of about $126 million in GDP in 2020 alone. Not that human beings' contributions should, of course, simply be measured in terms of their capacity to produce income. But the stats quantifying the overall economic impact of women's digital marginalisation are staggering. Furthermore, data measuring the repercussions of digital exclusion on women's educational and professional experiences are worrying. The United Nations, UNICEF and various national and international NGOs have all registered, although to different levels, difficulties in accessing online learning, work and other digital resources across the female population of many countries. And – surprise, surprise – they have noted that barriers to access often stem from a combination of gender and differences in class, race, physical ability and geography.

In Pakistan, for instance, women of all ages have had a hard time getting online during the pandemic. Just like in Kenya, they were hindered by a combination of gender stereotypes and economic inequalities. Electronic gadgets felt more costly than ever, with broadband being largely absent in several rural areas. Then, social norms have done the rest: in many Pakistani households young women's Internet use is viewed as particularly 'dangerous' or 'inappropriate', and girls were prevented from connecting during lockdowns.

'People here don't like the Internet for women. They say the Internet will ruin you,' said a Karachi-based student named Shazina, who had returned to live in her village during the pandemic, to the non-profit organisation Media Matters for Democracy (MMD). 'My attendance [in online classes] is not being marked. I haven't attended any class since the lockdown. There is an Internet connection in my house, but my family says don't use the Internet.'

Several other schoolgirls (and many adult women too) reported that the only devices in their households were being monopolised by their male relatives, or that they had no privacy to use them. 'I can't find much space, I can't attend online study circles and because it's a joint family system I have to do household chores,' said another young study participant to MMD researchers. Altogether, MMD concluded that out of ten surveyed Pakistani women, six had families that were restricting their access to the Internet.

Another fact worth noting is that media and humanitarian organisations have collected very similar testimonies in places as varied as India, Ethiopia, Vietnam, Peru, as well as in some of the G20's richest countries. Disabled women around the world have regularly been among the most affected groups, with their low connection rate preventing them from accessing services, sources of income and, above all, medical care. An equal disgrace is the lack of connection in many detention and migration centres, where female detainees, migrants and refugees (together with other people of all genders) have found themselves totally isolated due to the virus.

In the UK, while the overall number of non-Internet users has declined over time, UK-based women have consistently represented almost 60 per cent (a total of 1.97 million residents) of those excluded from technology use. According to government statistics, there are also gender disparities in digital skills: women, for instance, make up more than 60 per cent of UK residents having no basic digital skills. As expected, young women are, on average, more connected than their mothers and grandmothers. But this does not mean they all own a digital device, or that they had regular access to the Net during Covid, especially if they live in economically vulnerable households.

Just bear in mind that, among other data, in 2021 Ofcom estimated that 559,000 children in Britain had no Internet access at all, and that up to 1.8 million children in the country might not have a laptop or computer at home. And while these datasets may not be disaggregated by gender, we only have to juxtapose them to the digital gender gap figures I just highlighted to put two and two together.

I'd like to leave you with one last example. As you're reading it, keep in mind that this is happening in one of the richest countries in the world.

In autumn 2020, during the Covid pandemic, a picture was taken in the Californian city of Salinas that went viral globally. You might remember it. In it you see two Latina young girls sitting outside a Taco Bell fast-food restaurant. Wearing pink trainers on their feet, heads bent over their keyboards, they were trying to connect to the restaurant's Wi-Fi to attend their classes.

In California – where most Big Tech companies have their main headquarters – the digital exclusion picture is paradoxically even grimmer than the UK. One out of four students has no Internet access, while almost 20 per cent of them do not have laptops or other devices on which they can study remotely. In the USA as a whole, a large number of Black, Latina, migrant and refugee women do not have a private Internet connection. So the Salinas photo should definitely enrage us, but not really surprise us.

Later on, further details emerged about the girls in the photo, since many Americans did in fact feel outraged and organised fundraising. Their mother, Juana, had come to the United States as a migrant. In order to take care of her three daughters, Juana worked as a fruit picker and also sold ice cream on the street. In the rented room where they all lived and from which they risked eviction during the pandemic, there was no Internet access. Interviewed by the press, many Californian state school teachers confirmed that they had done their best to lend laptops and tablets to disadvantaged families during Covid. Too many schoolchildren, though, still had no way to learn online because vast urban zones do not have broadband.

I've got one more piece of data for you. Juana and her daughters lived a one-hour drive away from Silicon Valley, where, since the beginning of the pandemic, *Forbes* counted about 24 new billionaires, many of whom built their fortunes out of digital technology. Incidentally, *Forbes* also registered an exorbitant increase in the fortunes of some of the richest tech entrepreneurs on the planet, from Mark Zuckerberg to Jeff Bezos and Elon Musk.

* * *

The Covid-19 pandemic, as I said at the beginning of this chapter, acted as both a magnifying glass and a multiplier of social injustices. Our increasing reliance on digital tools exposed women like me, my friends and billions of social media, dating app and video call users to the risk of harassment and other unpleasant and sometimes traumatic experiences. It also allowed many organisations, beginning with tech companies and many employers, to exploit us all in novel and insidious ways, in our capacity as both workers and consumers. The more 'connected' we became, the longer we were asked to work, even though the virus was raging outside and at home, perhaps, a child needed our attention. Our increased 'connection' also made it all the more possible for our personal information to be extracted and manipulated to feed into digital companies' income, with little consideration for the consequences.

Of course, even pre-Covid, the question was never 'Digital is good? Digital is bad?' Still, we cannot be blind to the risks that the hyper-digitisation of the last couple of years has exposed us to, nor can we ignore their gendered dimension.

Men, in fact, have not been shielded from these trends either, but women have experienced them quite differently. Many took on the burden of care-related activities (many of which were also transferred online and became at times even more labour intensive). Meanwhile, women were also treated like cannon fodder by platforms who were perfectly aware that they were targeting us with harmful content and yet still bombarded us with it.

This is nothing new. Think of the dieting and plastic surgery sectors, which have a long history of capitalising on women's insecurities. Industries like tobacco, too, have often targeted women specifically, in the attempt to sell them harmful products. But things have now been taken to the next level. Social media companies involve even young girls in prosumption – i.e. indispensable to maintaining the digital economy engine, whatever the cost for those who might struggle with depression, anxiety or even an eating disorder.

Except that when we consider the other side of the coin – the digital gender gap still affecting a great proportion of the world's population – we notice a tragic paradox. For every woman who is violated or exploited through the use of digital technologies or while involved in tech production, there are many others who do not even have access to the Internet, or have less access than the men around them. And this has colossal repercussions on their future prospects. Rose's case – in a nutshell, that of a woman for whom a smartphone could have helped her be economically independent during lockdown and, perhaps, to report an abusive husband – is extremely telling for more than one reason. It demonstrates that, despite all their dark sides, communication technologies can still create opportunities for economic liberation, from which 'disconnected' women will remain excluded. And Rose's story also tells us that keeping women away from the Internet is becoming an effective way to maintain them in a subaltern position within the home. This risk is apparent in all the testimonies and figures that, all over the world, highlight the global shame of schoolgirls unable to attend online classes.

In terms of education, too, the pandemic has made a difference. During the last 25 years UNESCO had registered a slow but clear improvement in female education rates internationally. Yet today, the organisation believes that Covid has reversed that trend, with the digital gender gap endangering millions of girls' right to receive an education and undermining their chances to grow into economically and socially autonomous adults.

So this is really the heart of the matter. Once perceived as a luxury, digital tools have turned into life essentials, which the world around us expects us to be constantly able to use. They seemed even more vital when an exceptional health emergency confined us in our home for weeks, even months, at a time. And they are likely to be increasingly vital in the years to come. That is why the fight for digital gender justice must, in my opinion, include at least two inseparable aspects. One is the struggle against the many forms of violence and exploitation connected to patriarchal digital capitalism. And the other is the denunciation of the obscene inequalities in technology distribution. Inequalities that, as far as I am concerned, look even more monstrous whenever I look at the revenues of the digital economy machine.

CHAPTER 7

The politics of the digital revolution

In summer 2014, the ex-boyfriend of American indie game developer Zoë Quinn made public a lengthy blog in which he accused her of cheating on him, lying to him and sleeping with a journalist who wrote game reviews.

The piece went viral and hordes of Internet users – many of whom appeared to identify as gamers – targeted Zoë and other women in the industry with a level of brutality and synchronisation seldom seen on the Internet until then. Email and bank accounts were hacked, nude pictures, home addresses and private information shared, and ferocious death and rape threats sent out on all social media platforms. Zoë was forced into hiding. Feminist media critic Anita Sarkeesian, who had already been made a target for producing videos in which she took issue with the sexist portrayal of women in mainstream video games, had to cancel a talk after organisers were warned a mass shooting was planned. Other game developers, feminist commentators and journalists who had spoken in Zoë's and Anita's defence were also subjected to harassment, including attempted 'swatting' (hoax reports to emergency services causing an entire SWAT team to show up in full force at someone's home).

Harassers rallied behind the soon-to-be-famous hashtag #Gamergate and anonymously organised through forums on Reddit, 4chan and 8chan, as well as on social networks such as Twitter and YouTube. National and international observers, at least initially, struggled to wrap their heads around the story. Many news sites granted equal coverage to the abuse and to the protests of some video game fans, who, taking on social media themselves, claimed to be the controversy's real victims. They maintained Zoë Quinn and others had exaggerated the scale of the attacks against them, which the gamers said were the work of 'a few rotten apples' within the gaming community. They also argued that progressive journalists were demonising them and their hobby, describing games as being plagued by violence and bigotry and players as a bunch of immature, mostly white men, opposing any attempts to promote diversity and inclusivity.

But the forces behind Gamergate were obvious enough for those who chose to look for them.

A young, incendiary conservative commentator, London-based Milo Yiannopoulos, prominently positioned himself in the dispute. By his own admission, he had never much cared for video games and had never hesitated to define gamers as a 'unemployed saddos living in their parents' basements'. In 2014, however, he started to create unprecedented buzz around Gamergate as well as himself, leveraging his increasingly visible social media profiles and publishing articles with aptly chosen titles such as 'Feminist bullies are tearing the videogame industry apart'. In fact, Milo had just obtained a column on right-wing news outlet Breitbart, led by none other than Donald Trump's future chief strategist Steve Bannon. And, in their own words, both Milo and Bannon had identified in video gamers a demographic of 'rootless white males', ideal to recruit into the legions of pro-Trump activists they were forming online. The plan seemed to work a treat. By indefatigably tweeting against Zoë Quinn and in defence of her tormentors, Milo managed to spread ultra-conservative ideology among many youngsters who had until that point shown very little interest in politics.

They were not the only ones to exploit Gamergate for both personal and political purposes. Mike Cernovich, an American with a background in law and author of self-help books for men only, also tirelessly tweeted and blogged against Zoë and other women in the industry. Previously, he had been mostly known for his misogynistic writing, such as: 'How to choke a woman' and 'How to avoid false rape accusations' (I swear I am not making them up, you'll find them cited in the References), or social network posts such as 'Date rape does not exist'. His writing and posts had made him somewhat well known within the 'manosphere', a dark galaxy of masculinist sites and social media pages, filled with men's rights activists, pickup artists and incels (short for involuntary celibates, men who hate women because they feel rejected by them sexually). But during Gamergate he also turned into a full-time, right-wing activist, feeding his public more generic ultra-conservative discourse and advocating for online violence as a form of free speech and a necessary weapon in the fight against 'feminazis' and 'the regressive left' (as the alt-rights put it).

Fast forward only a couple of years and their efforts paid off.

Milo Yiannopoulos, Mike Cernovich and, notably, Steve Bannon emerged as three of the most recognisable figures of the alt-right, the slippery political force that backed Donald Trump in the 2016 US election, which mostly emerged online. Many gamergaters and manosphere users converged into this new political movement. And, in the meantime, the weaponisation of online violence for political ends reached unprecedented levels.

Mike Cernovich specialised in spreading disinformation on social media about Donald Trump's rival, Hillary Clinton. Milo Yiannopoulos incited his tens of thousands of social media followers against different yet carefully chosen women, enemies of the Trumpist movement, who fought for causes such as feminism, anti-racism and social justice. As for Steve Bannon, having successfully led the Trump election campaign, he installed himself in the White House as the new president's chief strategist. And Donald Trump himself, once elected, continued to follow the very same modus operandi as Cernovich, Yiannopoulos and Bannon. He regularly unleashed Internet users against female politicians, journalists and activists, including Democratic congresswomen Alexandria Ocasio-Cortez, Ilhan Omar and Rashida Tlaib. In a much talked about incident, he even falsely insinuated on Twitter that Ilhan Omar, a Muslim of Somali origin, had danced in celebration on the anniversary of 9/11. He exposed her to such a barrage of threats that the Capitol's guards had to review Ilhan's security protocol.

* * *

This all sounds interesting, Lilia, you may now be saying to yourself, *but you have been telling us how technology heightens gender injustices, while an entire economic system profits from it. So what does digital capitalism have to do with Bannon, Trump and the political weaponisation of online abuse?* The answer is: an awful lot, except that to fully understand this I need to add yet another layer to the analysis. We need, in particular, to ask ourselves what those who govern us do – or, rather, what they are presently *failing* to do – in order to address all of the problems, injustices and exploitation.

Online aggressions. Algorithmic bias. Violation of tech workers' rights. Unequal distribution of digital resources. Why on earth are political elites standing idly by amid the havoc (or at least why don't they intervene as rapidly and effectively as they should)?

Here's exactly where incidents such as Gamergate start providing us with at least some partial answers. One of the reasons why many governments have so far done relatively little in the face of digital capitalism's many problems is that politicians and governments play a part in all this, starting with online violence. The method tested in the English-speaking world during Gamergate has since spilled over into many different countries. I'll give you some examples.

When he was interior minister, Italian right-winger Matteo Salvini repeatedly exposed women who disagreed with or criticised him to online harassment. In a particularly controversial instance, his social media team (known to the Italian press as 'the beast') shared from the minister's official accounts a photo of three teenage female students, who were protesting his policies on the street. As was the intention, about 10,000 offensive or violent messages followed (what in Internet jargon is known as a 'shitstorm'). They included 'get raped', 'go and suck di*ks' and 'sell your body, at least you'll be worth something'. The same mechanism was deployed against other peaceful street protesters, as well as female writers and rival politicians. Former United Nations official and president of the Chamber of Deputies Laura Boldrini, whom Salvini once compared to an 'inflatable doll', was one of 'the beast's' favourite targets. So was German ship captain Carola Rackete, for having disobeyed the Italian government's order not to disembark in Sicily some refugees she had rescued at sea.

From Europe to Asia, the technique remains much the same. In India, a particularly horrifying case was that of investigative reporter Rana Ayyub, who authored an exposé of the Indian government's responsibility for anti-Muslim attacks in the state of Gujarat. She has since been hunted by members of Prime Minister Narendra Modi's political party. A regular recipient of hate speech on Twitter, Rana was also subjected to non-consensual pornography in 2018, when a 'deepfake'[4] porn video of her was circulated on WhatsApp, then Facebook, and shared over 40,000 times. As Rana threw up out of horror and mortification, she found out that her personal phone number had been posted on social media underneath a screenshot

4   Deepfakes are films produced through 'deep learning', an artificial intelligence method that allows computers to replicate convincingly on videos the movements of a face. For example, an adult performer in an existing porn scene can be digitally edited into the likeness of a woman of the creator's choosing – a celebrity, an ex, a classmate, a neighbour. All it takes is a (non-sexual) picture of her, easily found on social media public profiles. The differences to a genuine piece of footage are almost impossible to spot. A 2019 report from DeepTrace, a start-up specialising in tools to spot deepfakes, found a total of 14,678 deepfake videos online. 90 per cent were of a pornographic nature and 100 per cent of those posted on the world's top four deepfake porn sites featured women.

of the video. After receiving a storm of threatening text messages, she felt so ill that she had to be hospitalised.

Moving on to South America, Brazilian President Jair Bolsonaro has often instigated his Internet fans against certain women, such as journalist Patrícia Campos Mello. 'It's very personal. We tend to think that this is something that stays online, and it does not. It's increasingly mixed with real life and many online threats I received migrated to the real world,' said Patrícia to the Reuters Institute for the Study of Journalism in Oxford. 'I had people yelling at me, calling my phone number saying, "I'm going to punch you in the face" or people actually doxing me, telling people to go to places where I was going to confront me [*sic*]. I've had threats against my son.' Patrícia also explained that online violence against women, in her experience, is a formidable weapon used to silence female opponents and as an instrument to build an aura of machoistic invincibility around the male leaders who use it.

As Patrícia suggests, the approach is always the same. Some shrewd political operators identify a predominantly male constituency, normally belonging to the dominant ethnic group in that specific region. Then they tell these men that the cause of all their troubles, from their own personal insecurities to the state of the economy and society, is the women who expect to have rights (or it's 'gays', 'immigrants', 'minorities', and the organisations that protect those groups). Having offered their supporters a convenient scapegoat, these operators provide them with well-chosen heroes, namely the most machoistic and chauvinistic figures on the political spectrum. Finally, they select at regular intervals a specific woman who appears to personify all the scarecrows they have created, and release against her a mob of angry social media users. Through this expedient, they manage to both expand their support base and keep it in a state of constant excitement.

The similarities of these accounts in different countries should not be regarded as mere coincidences. After leaving the White House following disagreements with Donald Trump, Steve Bannon has kept close ties with the Bolsonaro family and European populist parties, and has always had words of appreciation for Modi's party's governing style. He has even attempted to launch a trans-continental political movement with a hub in Brussels and a global political communication school in Tuscany. During interviews and meetings with other right-wingers, he has spoken very frankly of the role played by digital harassment in the political manipulation techniques he wishes to spread. He has declared, for example, that the best way to mobilise political support on the Internet is to 'create chaos' and 'turn on hate', and that if women want to escape social media abuse, then all they have to do is 'switch off their computers'. He has even openly recognised the value of the Gamergate experience in clarifying this vision of his. Of video game fans, for instance, he has said unashamedly that 'You can activate that army. They came in through Gamergate or whatever and then get turned onto politics and Trump.'

In light of these revelations, then, it makes sense to go back to the questions raised at the beginning of this chapter. Because we should face the reality of the situation. For a few years now, some of the world's most powerful leaders have been using online misogyny as a weapon, and have even been exchanging tips about its deployment. Should we now expect them to rush to protect women's rights in the digital sphere? Should we expect them to legislate to remedy the worst sides of digital capitalism?

Plus, while the toxic relationship between technology, right-wing ideology and machoistic leaders is definitely part of the problem, there's another thing we should be constantly mindful of. And that is: it doesn't take a sit-down with Steve Bannon to understand that declaring an online war on women has political pay-offs. And you don't have to embrace right-wing values to contribute to that war.

Proof of this is that carefully orchestrated online attacks have recently been used by political groups and figures internationally regardless of where they stand on the right–left continuum. Do you remember the regular assaults on Jess Phillips MP, which I discussed in Chapter 1? You should know that while many are unleashed by ultra-conservatives, others originate within her own party.

Still, because it's the same the world over, in Vladimir Putin's Russia (which, as we all know, is quite hard to classify on the left–right spectrum) female dissidents fear the notorious 'web brigades'. This is software able to autonomously manage multiple fake accounts called bots, whose ultimate purpose is to create chaos and disinformation on behalf of Moscow and gag political dissidents within and outside national borders.

Among their targets, for example, is Poland's celebrated writer and co-founder of the feminist movement Women's Strike, Klementyna Suchanow, whom I am honoured to call a friend. Klementyna has often told me she is besieged by bots pretty much every time she speaks up online, particularly whenever she denounces the connections between the Kremlin and the pro-Russian, notoriously anti-women government in Warsaw.

Klementyna has also noticed that these bots are truly masterful when it comes to disseminating false and contradictory information. While being a well-known critic of Moscow's regime, she has a Russian-sounding name. Therefore, over the last few years, she has had various fake accounts regularly calling her a 'Russian bitch' and a 'Soviet agent'. And this was not simply meant to spread hate against her specifically. Trolling her, the brigades created chaos, polarised the Polish electorate and kept it in a state of perennial alarm.

'An investigative journalist has recently discovered a bot factory in a Polish town,' she said to me the last time she came to visit me in Naples, where I had invited her to speak about her work to fellow Italian activists. 'And this, apart from genuinely scaring me, has shown me that at this point our government has already learned a thing or two from Putin's digital experts.'

So here are some logical conclusions to be drawn from all these events taking place across the world. First, online hate is now methodically galvanised by figures of varying political backgrounds, who believe feeding women to the Internet wolves is an acceptable way to climb to power. And second, we should probably ask ourselves some serious questions about what we can expect from our politicians. And we should do so rather urgently.

* * *

Vladimir Putin and Jair Bolsonaro are, as we know, still in power. But neither Donald Trump nor Matteo Salvini are. However, this does not mean that the new governments of the USA and Italy rushed off to regulate digital capitalism and its patriarchal aspects the day they came to power. And this is a demonstration of how not everything starts and ends with single political leaders.

To shed some light on this, I will now share a few considerations inspired by three photos (you will find links to them in the References), which I selected by skimming through the diaries of prominent politicians.

In the first image, we can see Barack Obama at dinner with a bunch of tech gurus. It's 2011, and around him, in shirtsleeves, are Apple's founder Steve Jobs, together with a very young Mark Zuckerberg and the then Google CEO Eric Schmidt. It is an iconic photo, because it epitomises the very tight links between the Obama White House and Silicon Valley, which earned the Democratic leader the nickname 'Tech President'. Over the following years, the Obama administration maintained especially close contacts with Google. Suffice it to say that according to recent estimates from the non-profit news organisation The Intercept, 55 of the corporation's former employees migrated to the federal government during Obama's two terms, while 197 government staffers went to work for Google, with representatives of the two organisations meeting at least 90 times in 2014 alone.

Picture number two was taken on a sunny day in the summer of 2016. In it, smiley as ever, is Italy's then prime minister, Matteo Renzi, and Amazon's then CEO (now executive chairman) Jeff Bezos, who was received with great fanfare by the Italian government in Rome. In 2016–18, a former senior vice president of Amazon, Diego Piacentini, had been appointed commissioner for digital innovation within Renzi's cabinet, and Jeff Bezos himself had congratulated all those involved with a celebratory tweet. And here's a real treat for political gossip aficionados: Amazon's number one wasn't the only tech entrepreneur Matteo Renzi had been determined to invite to Italy. During that same summer, he hosted Mark Zuckerberg in Rome, presenting him with a special gift: a copy of Cicero's *De Amicitia* (meaning 'On Friendship') (the volume's title hinted at the idea of sending a friend request on Facebook and it seems Meta's founder is fond of Latin).[5]

Let's move on to picture number three. Left to right: Google's CEO Pichai Sundararajan; Saudi prince, Mohammed bin Salman; and Google's co-founder and former Alphabet president Sergey Brin. It's 2018, they're in California, and the three men are giving the camera a toothy smile. They met to discuss a potential cloud computing collaboration between Google and the Saudi government (in spite of multiple warnings from human rights organisations such as Amnesty International, alarmed by the Saudi regime's appalling record in matters of digital surveillance and political use of technology against dissident voices).

These three photos tell us many things. The first is that, especially in the 2010s, there was no global leader who'd miss a photo op with a tech guru. And that wasn't simply because the digital entrepreneurs' 'youthful' and 'informal' style and the 'innovative' and 'cool' aura surrounding their firms helped freshen the image of sometimes lacklustre (and sometimes morally compromised) political

5   While perhaps less notable, there are also plenty of photos showing the tight relationship between UK politicians and tech entrepreneurs. Some of the most talked about were taken at the Technology Entrepreneurs Reception hosted at 10 Downing Street by David Cameron in October 2015 (see links to the photos in the References). You'll notice that while a few women can be spotted in the room, the vast majority of the attendees were men.

establishments. Businesses like Google, Microsoft and Apple created and still create new jobs globally (although, as we already know, not always well-protected or justly remunerated ones). And, as we've seen, in various cases they also offer support, resources and advice to governments' own agencies.

Quite naturally, though, these ties have made political elites very vulnerable to tech companies' lobbying, and extremely reluctant to intervene and regulate digital capitalism. If you need further proof of this, look no further than another political hot potato most governments haven't yet managed to sort out: the regulation of online election advertising. I assume many of you will remember the scandal that followed revelations surrounding the activities of the now defunct UK consultancy Cambridge Analytica. If you don't, let me quickly remind you what it was all about.

Starting in 2013, Cambridge Analytica harvested information from millions of social media users (often without their permission) and used it to help candidates worldwide 'micro-target' political ads. Among the elections apparently influenced by the consultancy's involvement were, famously, the Brexit referendum in 2016 and the US presidential election won by Donald Trump that same year. And while these malpractices caused great malaise and made people reflect perhaps more thoroughly than ever before on how data mining, algorithms and social media may influence and even distort the inner workings of democracy, most countries still lack stringent legislation on online propaganda. Might this be to do with the fact that almost all political groups use to their advantage the very same technologies they'd be called to regulate? Certainly worth thinking about.

Lastly, in the interests of fairness, it must be said that several important reforms on digital matters are currently being discussed, some of which are very close to approval or even implementation.[6] As already discussed, parliamentary investigations have recently been conducted on the practices of porn tubes and the treatment of social media moderators, and several measures have been adopted in areas as different as conflict minerals, online violence and disinformation on social media. As I write, in the UK as well as in the EU some pioneering legislation is also under discussion which specifically pertains to online safety, digital propaganda and digital monopolies. I have to admit, though, that I struggle to think of even a single legal intervention that hasn't been long hindered or slowed down by tech firms' lobbying and by the political establishments' inner tensions.

On one side, we generally find combative groups led, as it happens, by progressive women: members of the US Democratic left such as Alexandria Ocasio-Cortez and Elizabeth Warren, as well as female civil servants within the EU Commission, and prominent targets of online abuse, including Jess Phillips. These are women who share a critical view of Big Tech platforms and strive to push the institutions they are part of to make strides on digital rights issues.

The problem is, however, that confusion reigns on the opposite side. Ironically, some right-wing populists have also lately turned against tech giants, especially in cases where corporations have taken even minimal measures to tackle online abuse or disinformation. There is one case above all the others: having been defeated by Joe Biden, Donald Trump himself made considerable use of Twitter

6   Among these, the UK's Online Safety Bill (mostly focusing on the prevention of online harm) and two EU legislative proposals (the Digital Markets Act and the Digital Services Act). (I shall return to all these in Part 3.)

and Facebook to incite his followers to attack Washington DC's Capitol in January 2021. Banned by both platforms, he has become a sworn enemy of social media companies and now loudly asks for platforms to be made liable for users' damages, which has created further chaos in the public debate.

So, building alliances for tech reform has become even harder within many governments. And while the titans of global tech might not be as universally popular as they used to be, they have hardly lost their place at the table and continue to have ample room for manoeuvre. Throughout the world, the laws we so desperately need are introduced painfully slowly, or, worse still, stalled or postponed to the next election cycle, when, perhaps, the government will have got its budget through, or consolidated its majority, and women's grievances will finally be given a minimal degree of attention. And we already know who will be caught in the middle in the meantime.

* * *

I am certain it wasn't lost on you that in the three photos I just described there is one woman visible. (To be fair, two women seem to have been invited to Barack Obama's tech dinner, one of whom can be seen in the photo: Yahoo's former CEO Carol Bartz. Yet they were the only ones at an otherwise men-only table.) Sadly, this is fairly representative of what happens the world over.

We badly need more courageous approaches to tech politics: tougher regulations, and effective measures against online gender-based violence and women's exploitation within the tech supply chain. So who's in the legislative bodies that should be adopting these approaches and introducing these measures? Globally, three quarters of these people are men (in some countries male legislators are no less than 80 per cent of the total).

Now, far be it from me to suggest that the presence of female lawmakers always, in itself, ensures feminist-friendly policy outcomes. There have been and are plenty of women who climbed to power but did not necessarily act in the interest of their sisters, Margaret Thatcher for instance. Nonetheless, the fact remains that it is overwhelmingly men who walk the corridors of power. Men who can change, with the stroke of a pen, the course of millions of women's lives, without ever having experienced the problems the other half of the global population is facing.

It was all men, for example, who populated yet another telling photo, taken in Alabama in 2019. It captures a session of the state senate, when 25 Republican men passed new, tighter anti-abortion legislation. It was all men that met in 2017 to discuss cuts to maternity benefits all over the United States. (In both cases, images were proudly posted online by some of the – male – lawmaker participants.) And it is, for instance, mostly (although not exclusively) men that make up the membership of Justice for Men and Boys (J4MB), a UK party which, among other things, advocates for cutting funds to encourage women to take on technology careers, and for ending gender equality policies at work and in decision-making bodies. (It should be noted that J4MB has never secured any parliamentary seats. Its very existence, however, is indicative of the lurking opposition to women's attempts to challenge their under-representation in both politics and tech-related fields.)

So what is the impact of this systematic marginalisation on the progressive economic and tech reforms I have been talking about? What does the daily life of a woman lawmaker willing to fight to make technology more just and more inclusive look like? Due to my advocacy work in gender and digital justice, I have met several of them, so I can share what I have learned.

Many of the female legislators I have found myself interacting with bravely engage in battles on, say, online hate speech, non-consensual pornography and female workers' rights, at national or European level. The vast majority attempt to maintain a relationship with feminist activists and experts like myself. During meetings between lawmakers and advocates and activists, these women diligently take notice of our concerns and suggestions, promising they will do their best to represent us. Almost all of them, however, face difficulties not unlike those encountered by the tech industry's women we met in previous chapters. Many are, for example, isolated figures, lacking the party support they need to work on all these problems more systemically. Others are exhausted, upset by the casual sexism that permeates their own workplaces. And in the end, we shake hands and finish our coffee, and off we all go, trying to do our best in our respective fields.

Finally, should you still have questions about the other side of this issue, that is to say, how the tech industry relates to these overwhelmingly male, largely exclusionary political elites, I have a last story for you, and it's a rather exemplary one.

Let us return for a moment to how Google/Alphabet's big shots happily let themselves be photographed with Saudi prince Mohammed bin Salman. And let us remember that this blue-blooded politician personifies not only the epitome of masculinist power, but also a regime ready to ferociously punish women who dare to rebel. You should know, in fact, that the crown prince is a vehement opponent of feminism, and that according to several humanitarian organisations he has ordered the arrest and torture of dozens of Saudi women activists. There is a reason why I have mentioned his links with Google: beyond talking business with him, the Californian corporation has even indirectly facilitated his administration's misogynistic practices.

This happened in 2015, when an app called Absher was developed by the Saudi government to help citizens access government services. As luck would have it, though, the device also enabled Saudi men to monitor the movements of their wives, daughters and sisters, all subjected, by order of the Saudi government, to the direct authority of male relatives. In particular, the application maintained a historical record of women's travelling and allowed male guardians to suspend, with a click or a tap, previously issued travel permissions.

The app could easily be downloaded from Google's and Apple's online stores. Saudi women's rights activists, NGOs like Amnesty International and Human Rights Watch and American and European female politicians of Muslim faith all heavily criticised the two tech corporations. They accused them of endorsing a legal and administrative system that subjugated women and treated them as second-class citizens, and urged them to take an unapologetic stance against the human rights violations enabled by their technologies.

Needless to say, the two companies said they'd look into it, but refused to adopt a firm position. A little while later, Google announced its decision to keep Absher in its store, on the grounds that it did not constitute a violation of its app store terms of use, and it continues to be available on Apple's online store.

So, these are the two fundamental aspects of the problem: tech firms support the least noble of political endeavours, and politicians turn a blind eye to the darkest sides of the digital revolution. And vice versa, over and over again, with men controlling both politics and tech, and often isolated and, at times, actively persecuted women sweating blood to make a change. It's sadly all too familiar.

* * *

Yet again, the system is chasing its own tail. And yet again, the problem is both similar and different to others we faced in past decades.

To begin with, today's muddled relationship between politics and Big Tech mirrors the stance political elites have taken with economic issues. We do not need to look that far back to make sense of the start of this. During the last 40 years of neoliberal ideology, our political institutions have undergone a profound crisis. Wild deregulation and privatisation measures have disseminated in half of the world a culture that discourages even the most timid redistribution policies and, more generally, any state intervention in the economy. (The state machine remains, unfortunately, a force to be reckoned with in other and less benign contexts, such as police repression of legitimate protests, but that's not what I'm looking at here.) To all this, add that financial shocks and economic recessions have further eroded the legitimacy of those who govern us – something that has given rise, in many countries, to exceptionally low voter turnout and even lower trust in governments and institutions. Increasingly distant from their citizens and increasingly unable to defend them from the wide repercussions of economic troubles, politicians have sought refuge in intense, ambiguous relationships with the world's biggest businesses. And this is true across the political spectrum: from Bill Clinton in the USA to Italy's Silvio Berlusconi and France's Emmanuel

Macron. In the UK, Peter Mandelson, a key figure in Tony Blair's election and government, famously declared that the 1990s' Labour Party leadership had no issues with company executives 'getting filthy rich'.

Rivers of ink have been devoted to all this by intellectuals, activists and journalists alike; I'll simply build on their analyses to summarise one of the greatest political tragedies of our times: the frantic, urgent need to make key political economic decisions, and our political machineries' sheer inability to make them. Decisions necessary, say, to stop global warming, to address increased socioeconomic inequalities following the Covid-19 pandemic, and to arrest violence and exploitation within patriarchal digital capitalism. Yet with few (however laudable) exceptions our leaders are inactive, unresponsive and, overall, are inadequate.

In light of this, the fact that we know the capitalistic and patriarchal logics are so tightly intertwined, there is a last obstacle we should always bear in mind. And that obstacle is the sexist DNA infused into our political and legal systems, which hinders the struggles of our (few) allies within political institutions. Think again of all those men-only photos: men making decisions about the lives of women they have never met, or at times refusing to decide anything whatsoever until it is far too late. Men in politics cosying up to men in tech; men in tech cosying up to men in politics. For these are mostly boys' clubs.

Now, add to this the sexist traits of the legal frameworks that should provide the bases for reforms, which are often biased against women and other historically oppressed groups. After all, it is only very recently that UK law has started to treat women as fully autonomous beings, rather than as men's economic property, but several legally sanctioned forms of gender injustice persist to this day. We cannot disregard how this historical legacy risks affecting technology-related legislation.

By closing the second part of the book on such a bitter note, it is not at all my intention to suggest that we should give up in despair, or ignore the significance of existing struggles to reclaim tech for liberation. If anything, I am proposing that we honour this ongoing resistance by acknowledging the harsh conditions in which it has developed.

Having made it clear that we are in the business of moving mountains, let us consider a few insights on how to actually *succeed* in moving them.

PART 3

What is to be done?

CHAPTER 8

Stealing the master's tools

If you had happened to pass by the gates of Newnham College (a women-only college within the University of Cambridge) on 8 March 2015, you would have come across more people than usual. Former students, lecturers, friends of friends, brought there by the power of word of mouth, arrived in dribs and drabs, and some visitors stopped to ask the porters where to find the 'hackathon'. Many of these women had never met each other, but they were preparing to celebrate International Women's Day together. And they were getting ready to celebrate it by 'hacking' one of the most visited websites in the world: Wikipedia.

Often cited as an example of successful social technology, the virtual encyclopedia has many virtues: its articles can, in principle, be edited by anyone, it is managed collectively and more or less democratically, and it is not profit-oriented. Too bad that, social technology or not, it seems to have long been rife with sexism. According to a 2021 study, less than 17 per cent of Wikipedia pages are devoted to women. This dramatic under-representation remains on the other side of the screen too: starting from the platform's launch, the number of women involved in editing has fluctuated slightly, but has never reached more than 20 per cent of total editors.

And to make matters worse, research in 2021 (see References) revealed that a specific type of prejudice has been ingrained for years in the Wikipedians' community: women's pages have often been hastily proposed for cancellation, as they were considered 'insufficiently notable'.[7] As a consequence, extraordinary female figures have been excluded from one of the main information sources on the planet, and millions of Internet users (students, journalists, random people in the grip of curiosity) have been presented with information almost exclusively filtered by the male gaze.

But on that day in March 2015, Newnham's women decided to reverse this injustice. This is why, for the entire afternoon, they put together bio after bio, Wiki page after Wiki page, flooding the website with new entries dedicated to women painters, thinkers, scientists, activists and their contributions to human civilisation.

They were not the only ones to commemorate International Women's Day in such a unique manner. As they edited the platform from England, a network of female researchers, programmers and artists simultaneously edited it from California. And so on and so

---

7   In 2018, the case of Nobel prize-winning physicist Donna Strickland attracted particular attention. While her co-author and co-winner Gérard Mourou had had his own Wikipedia page since 2005, the professor's biography was approved only after her award was announced. Before then, a page devoted to her had been rejected by editors on the grounds that it didn't meet the criterion of 'notability'.

forth, a total of about 80 groups of improvised feminist hackers across the world. Thanks to these types of activities, Wikipedia entries have appeared that remember women such as Rosa Lee Ingram, an icon of the American civil rights movement, and to organisations such as the Sojourners for Truth and Justice, which in the 1950s fought for the rights of African American women and communities. They were dutifully given their rightful place, ready to inspire present and future generations.

It is worth mentioning that this hacking marathon was not a onc-off initiative. Since 2015, many universities, museums and foundations have regularly hosted similar events, coordinating with each other from one country to the next, with many women editing from homes and offices, supporting the efforts of those who had joined the live events.

Altogether, it is estimated that about 17,000 new women-centred pages have been inserted into Wikipedia as a result of these endeavours, which is impressive, isn't it? I can already foresee some of your more than legitimate comments: *So what's this all about? After having told us page after page that we are dealing with massive, circular, extremely complex problems, you are now trying to persuade us that to solve them it is enough to just go and hack Wikipedia? That if we organise and reclaim bits and pieces of the Web, all the rest will simply follow?*

And the answer is: yes and no. Yes, I will attempt to convince you that sometimes it is possible to subvert digital technologies from within, rectifying sexist discriminations and other forms of injustice. And no, I don't believe that will be enough to break the many vicious circles we have explored so far. Precisely because I think other strategies are also necessary, I will offer in Chapter 9 a series of political and policy proposals which may push us in the right direction. I am also persuaded, though, that all the political and policy proposals in the world won't do much good unless we first let ourselves be inspired by a positive vision of a different technology for the future. And I don't mean a banal perspective, such as 'digital technology can also be used for good', because this has never been in dispute.

We have already seen, however, how technology is anything but neutral, and is, instead, involved in intricate webs of violence and exploitation. So it is more than understandable to doubt that we may be able to reappropriate it for liberation. Or to fear – to quote Black American poet and feminist activist Audre Lorde – that 'the master's tools will never dismantle the master's house'. For what will we do if the master takes those tools back? What if digital technologies rebel against us and, instead of utilising them to emancipate and resist, we find ourselves caught in the very oppressive mechanisms we wanted to demolish?

In this chapter, I will admit in all honesty that these risks are real and serious. But I will also try to show that if we steal the tools away from the master, and if we transform them to make them our own, we can aspire to demolish at least a wall of the master's house. Then, who knows, that might prove to be a load-bearing wall. And from the ruins, we might be able to recover useful materials to build differently, and better, with a brand-new toolkit.

* * *

It is not only me, of course, who has been thinking about reclaiming technology to disrupt gender injustices. The very first person to embrace this vision was probably Canadian-American writer and activist Shulamith Firestone, who in the 1960s and 70s had been asking herself whether digital developments could alleviate gender disparities in the future. About two decades later, the debate was reopened by celebrated philosopher Donna Haraway, largely thanks to the publication of her influential essay entitled 'A Cyborg Manifesto', considered the cornerstone of so-called cyber-feminist thought. Simplifying to the extreme, I'd say the manifesto rotated around one central argument. Although admitting that, historically, technology had been shaped by capitalism and other oppressive logics, it proposed that digital tools might have been converted to an emancipatory purpose, helping make differences between men and women a little more fluid and a little less divisive.

If this seems optimistic to you, you need to consider that almost 40 years have passed, which means we are now all too aware of the many ways in which the digital revolution betrayed the promises that had been made to women. And broken promises do hurt. But it is equally true that, in many cases, women have managed to push digital technology towards the direction indicated by cyber-feminists. In other words, they have turned them into a hammer to smash stereotypical conceptions of gender and other power dynamics. The Wikipedia hackathon is a case in point. I'm going to share three more examples now, which I have chosen for their special relevance.

The first example has to do with all virtual reality forms allowing us to experiment with different gender identities. I am talking about video games, augmented reality simulations and other virtual universes, where participants can see the world through the eyes of someone from a different gender. Not that this means that every video game with female characters can kick-start a feminist revolution, of course.

Proof of this is the famous game *Tomb Raider*, through which millions of players put themselves in the shoes of protagonist Lara Croft. Lara, however, was depicted to be so conventionally alluring (and, at the same time, with so little psychological depth) that many gamers, by their own admission, ended up focusing mostly on the graphics' voyeuristic effects.

Nevertheless, if we move away from mainstream products to indie games, perhaps designed by women or queer people, things become much more interesting. A video game called *Mainichi* has been so appreciated by feminist and LGBTQ+ movements that it has often been cited as a case study in university courses in gender studies. It was created by developer Mattie Brice, herself a transgender woman, who got the idea for the game by thinking about her own daily life. In Japanese, *mainichi* means 'on a daily basis' and the game takes you through a day in the life of a trans woman. It is undoubtedly a very instructive game. Should you download it (which you can do for free), you'll discover that if your avatar chooses to spend more time putting on make-up and emphasising her femininity, she will be constantly harassed in the street or at the restaurant. If, instead, she focuses less on her looks, she will have to face other humiliating incidents, including being repeatedly mistaken for a man.

One more telling detail: Mattie created *Mainichi* using a freeware, which means, as I mentioned above, that the game can be played for free. As if to say: apart from destabilising sexism and prejudices, why not try to shake the monopoly of big gaming brands a little? With this in mind, Mattie killed two birds with one stone: she raised awareness within the gaming community around women's and queer people's rights, and she empowered as many people as possible to ask themselves important questions regarding gender norms and their social and existential implications.

That being said, other liberating experimentations have been started from more mainstream technologies, which had not been designed with gender justice purposes in mind. After all, every now and then even the master lets his guard down, and advantage can be taken of the opportunity.

Have you heard of Tumblr, a micro-blogging platform started in 2007, initially very popular and then gradually forgotten after having been purchased by Yahoo? Well, before the change of ownership, Tumblr was famous for the progressive values of its users, and most notably for its popularity within the LGBTQ+ community. Many transgender bloggers used it to document their transition process, and other sexual and gender minorities had identified it as a 'safe space' to discuss their life experiences and to educate others. Various independent adult performers, who often identified themselves as queer, were also using Tumblr to channel a more inclusive eroticism, far from the exploitative and homogenising dynamics typical of mainstream online porn.

Yet this libertarian atmosphere didn't last for long. Yahoo, and later Verizon (which bought Yahoo in 2017), banned all such materials from the platform, first preventing the use of tags which made them more easily retrievable and then censoring them completely. From one day to the next, even pictures showcasing bodies following transition surgeries could be censored as 'obscene' and 'offensive'. As a result, Tumblr's queer users soon migrated on to other sites, and the platform's culture changed considerably. A couple of years later, Tumblr was sold to a third tech company, Automattic, this time at a fraction of its original value.

Not that the speculations of one tech firm or another are particularly relevant to our discussion, but a few things must be said at the very least. Tumblr, in truth, was hardly perfect. Like the vast majority of social media platforms, it also hosted abuse and digital attacks, as well as questionable advertising practices, such as using bots programmed to spam its users. To refer back to Audre Lorde's words, it was a tool designed and controlled by the master. Still, for a short while, that tool was used from below in a genuinely emancipatory manner. Historically oppressed groups used it to frame a less constrictive representation of gender, to do self-organised sex education and to advance an independent, more honest and ethical pornography than that which fills the greatest part of the Internet. And nowadays, I'd say that's quite something.

To continue to follow this line of reasoning, example three is also connected to a tool provisionally stolen away from the master. Except this time, the master seriously struggled to take it back.

Some of you might perhaps be familiar with the controversies surrounding the ultra-famous doll Barbie: the blonde and slender doll that generations of little girls have adored and continue to do so, while also making them feel insecure and inadequate, as they compare their body, life and wardrobe to their toy's rarefied world. Mattel, the multinational behind Barbie, has attempted over the last few years to silence these criticisms by giving its doll a feminist restyling. Among its various initiatives, the company launched an ebook entitled *Barbie: I Can Be a Computer Engineer.*

Initially, the publication was announced as a great step forward. Finally, an inspiring role model of a woman in tech! Viva Barbie! Viva the girls who will read about her adventures and will want to study engineering! Except the Barbie of the ebook had very little in common with the average engineer. A couple of cheesy illustrations showed her as she let her little sister's computer get infected by a virus, only to then ask (male) friends to help her repair the damage. All smiles, she would then reveal to the reader that she only cares about 'design': she was happy to leave coding and other hard stuff to the men among the aspiring engineers.

Partially out of frustration and partially resolved to turn this book into an opportunity for debate, it was a real-life Californian software engineer Kathleen Tuite who saved the day. In no time, Kathleen launched a platform called Feminist Hacker Barbie, from which Internet users could have fun hacking Mattel's book, replacing the original pages with new text and images depicting Barbie as a skilful programmer. Thousands of people accepted Kathleen's witty invitation ('Barbie's new book tells girls they need boys to code for them. Help Barbie be the competent, independent, bad-ass engineer that she wants to be') and rewrote the ebook's story, sharing their creations on social media and bombarding Mattel's accounts with sarcastic messages.

Bottom line: the company's PR operation had failed, the book was withdrawn from the market and for many days the Internet discussed how to encourage less obsolete representations of gender and technology. Just a drop in the ocean, maybe? Once again, my answer to this is that we desperately need drops such as these, which can provide us with precious lessons for the future.

First, it is possible to use digital technologies not to oppress but to liberate, not to subjugate but to support the resistance. Then, yes, within this ongoing oppression–resistance circuit, the devices we have reclaimed might be reconverted to their original function. Just like in the case of Tumblr, where the time of sexual liberation and gender experimentation was only too brief, yet it did happen, and that's the point.

Second lesson: these attempts to occupy increasingly wider areas of the Web (social networks, the gaming sector, digital marketing campaigns and the like) should at times be carried out creatively and, let me add, light-heartedly. Have fun with it, while we very legitimately keep exploring what alternatives there might be to the master's house, as we remain trapped within its very walls. Fighting tooth and nail, attempting to regain some degree of freedom and subjectivity, we need to continue our efforts. And it seems that when it comes to affirming our freedom and subjectivity, to preserve the energy that is necessary for the fight, very few things are as effective as creativity, fun and pleasure.

This is why I warmly recommend you give thanks to feminist hackers wherever they might be and enjoy as much as you can their most radical and playful provocations. And, meanwhile, I invite you to keep an eye on the trends I'm going to discuss next.

* * *

Suppose you were a woman eager to make her corner of the world a tiny bit better, and were in need of support, advice and resources. Or suppose that, whatever your gender, you wanted to know more about the campaigns, social projects and community work carried out by women from different countries and support their endeavours. You'd probably start by collecting some information online. And since it's not always easy to orient ourselves in the Web's labyrinth, you might begin with a couple of quick Google searches, or skimming through relevant content on Facebook or YouTube. And that, of course, would not necessarily be a bad idea.

But I will suggest an alternative option, which I hope might offer you some food for thought regarding the issue I highlighted at the beginning of this chapter: how do we create new toolkits? I suggest you check out an independent, non-commercial, women-only social network called World Pulse.

In the early 2000s, World Pulse was a magazine, which specialised in women's stories. Its creator, US journalist Jensine Larsen, founded it after having travelled across several continents to collect women's testimonies, documenting their problems and struggles. During her travels, Jensine became convinced that new spaces were needed, where women could take centre stage, support one another and share their stories on their own terms. From that intuition, a new, highly original platform was born, grounded in one principle only: global sisterhood.

As I write, all those who identify as a woman can open a profile on World Pulse and use it to form solidarity ties with about 80,000 other users registered on the site, coming from over 220 countries, who are mostly socially or politically engaged. Not even language barriers are that relevant, since the portal has an automatic translator facilitating conversations. In other words, any visitor can launch calls for action, enhancing the visibility of her local initiatives, and making her skills and networks available to others. This is how, for instance, a Canadian woman, Tam, met a Nigerian woman, Olanike, and together they started a training programme on environmental issues involving thousands of African girls. This is how Tiffany Brar, an Indian community organiser with a visual disability, started to spread internationally best practices on making online content more accessible to disabled people. And this is how Neema Namadamu, a Congolese feminist, funded and opened a media centre specialising in digital skills training and digital activism, named Maman Shujaa ('Hero Women' in Swahili). Within the centre's structure, women and girls from the Democratic Republic of the Congo (many of whom are survivors of the horrifying violence described in Chapter 3) can learn digital skills that help them to study, work and, above all, organise to defend their rights. Neema founded it after her own 25-year-old daughter had been attacked by a Congolese national militia. Within World Pulse's community she found professional connections, technical assistance and many allies ready to help her spread the word about her project.

It's important to note that World Pulse purposefully chose not to comply with the organisational and economic models dominant within digital capitalism. For example, unlike mainstream social networks, it uses data extracted from the website visits only to improve its services, and funds itself through donations rather than algorithmically targeted ads. Women like Tam, Olanike, Tiffany and Neema are therefore able to use the portal while limiting the risks connected to traditional social networks.

That said, more than understandably, every now and then World Pulse, too, uses tools coming straight from the master's toolkit, starting from its Facebook account, utilised to share the most important updates from World Pulse's community, or its agreement with Google Translate to secure the simultaneous translation of the interactions between its members.

Yet a different tool (an ethical, feminist one, inspired by values that oppose those of the master) is now being circulated.[8] And, as you're about to discover, what's also being circulated is a series of methods to produce more.

* * *

To claim back, hack or occupy existing technologies is, as we've seen, both possible and productive. Still, creating brand-new tools from scratch, such as World Pulse (thought out from day one to mirror social and gender justice values), is perhaps an even more fascinating prospect. So, you should know that there are plenty of networks of women designers, coders and technologists committed to this endeavour.

Before telling you more, however, I'd like to render to Caesar the things that are Caesar's. That is to say, to mention how feminist tech design approaches are indebted to yet another rich tradition

---

8   Beyond World Pulse, there are several other examples of non-profit platforms. One of the most notable is All Out, a digital community specialising in petitions and crowdfunding in support of LGBTQ+ individuals and organisations. Another key difference between All Out and the various commercial websites of this kind (see Change.org) is that All Out relies on a multinational and multilingual experts team, whose task is to liaise with LGBTQ+ grassroots activists globally. Having collaborated with All Out in the past, I am a witness to its extraordinary efficacy, which led, among other things, to the funding of a Berlin-based centre assisting Muslim queer people, and to the evacuation of sexual minorities subjected to kidnap, torture and possible execution in Chechnya.

of political and technological experimentation: disability rights movements. For decades, activists with disabilities have fought for a social, critical approach to technology design. I'd say the reasons for this are obvious enough. On the one hand, the vast majority of technologies are generally created without taking into account the needs of people with disabilities, who are often made invisible within our societies. On the other hand, paradoxically, even in cases where a device is specifically developed with disabled users in mind, people with disabilities are seldom included in the creative process and are often stereotyped based on discriminatory or patronising attitudes. Sound familiar?

I am not equating, logically, the silencing of people with disabilities (regardless of their gender) to the silencing of women (who might or not be disabled). But it seems rather clear to me that there are some similarities in the way both groups are treated when it comes to tech design. Think of how many tech companies ignore the specific needs of women, starting from the need to be safe from online violence. Think of cases such as that of Mattel's ebook, where the idea of a 'women-friendly' product is no more than a trivialising marketing operation. And precisely as a result of such similarities, women learned a thing or two from disability justice activists. For a start, they learned to strive for participatory design projects, ensuring the constant involvement of all constituencies which will benefit from a given device. And they also learned to convey the idea that when we pay attention to the voices of the user community greater innovation may emerge. For, so they say, necessity is the mother of invention. And if those who experience a necessity have the opportunity to speak up and elaborate strategies that make sense to them and fit their needs, those strategies will probably be the very best, and might provide ways to address future problems.[9]

Except in this case, too, we must pay attention. As I've already mentioned, there are many examples, under the pretence of 'meeting women's needs', of companies simply engaging in marketing or trying to target a market niche. Let us take, for example, the pink, 'feminine' laptops, smartphones and coding kits that cyclically fill stores. (I have nothing against pink or any other colour, but I think we can agree that the problems we are discussing call for rather different interventions.) Or the so-called 'period apps' – applications that enable the monitoring of one's menstrual cycle or pregnancy and are at times celebrated as instances of feminist design. The problem, however, is that some of these apps have adopted such ambiguous data-mining policies they outdo those of the usual social networks. Suffice it to say that the Flo menstrual app has recently been accused of sharing with Facebook and Google extremely private users' information, including their ovulation dates, without – it seems – asking for their permission.

You've got the picture. Products and tools sold as models of feminist design often turn out to be mere 'pinkwashing': a form of appropriation of feminist ideas and languages that has little to do with actual feminism. The fact remains, though, that thankfully

9   Among the most notable examples of this mechanism is the invention of the first typewriter prototype, created by Italian inventor Pellegrino Turri and his friend (and probably lover) Carolina Fantoni, who had started to lose her sight. In order to continue exchanging affectionate letters, the duo developed a machine based on the mechanical skills of the former and the daily experience of the latter. This story is often cited in the writings of disability rights activists, for example Haben Girma, the first deafblind person to graduate from Harvard Law School.

there are several examples of design and technology production grounded in feminist values and democratic inclusion. I will give you a couple of examples.

The first is a collaboration between Briton Charlotte Webb (co-founder of the Feminist Internet campaign) and the Australian artist and designer Josie Young. Over the last few years, Charlotte and Josie have put together a list of criteria, questions and procedures that those seeking to create 'AI feminist systems' should bear in mind. Criteria and questions such as: 'Rather than design for a "universal user", can you identify a stakeholder who is not currently well served, and who could benefit from your design? [...] What different participatory methods do you have available so that your stakeholder can co-create or have direct input into the development of your design? Some examples include [...] having a stakeholder from the community that you are designing for on your design team [...] co-creation design workshops, early and ongoing feedback and testing.'

They asked whether creators have considered: 'How your values and position might lead you to choose one option over another [...]? How will you collect and treat data through the development of your design? [...] How will you minimise the carbon and climate footprint of your design? [...] Where might unpaid or exploited labour exist in the production/supply chain of the technology you're using?'

Based on such considerations, Josie and Charlotte created some new feminist AI tools, including two chatbots. In practice, this is software programmed to simulate human conversation. (You know the automatic responders used on the customer service section on websites? Imagine this converted into feminist bots.) The first chatbot is named F'xa and its goal is to offer a mostly youthful audience information on the topic of algorithmic bias. The second, Maru, has been launched in partnership with NGO Plan International, a global authority on matters of girls' rights, and aims to provide information and tips on digital violence prevention. Both systems have been co-created with young activists (teenagers from Benin, Cameroon, Germany, Ghana, the UK, Nepal and South Africa were all involved in Maru's development). And – not an insignificant point – neither chatbot mines data from interactions with users.

Other intriguing models can be borrowed from the many collectives of feminist makers and hackers, many of which, beyond experimenting with coding, reflect together on how to bring feminism into tech and technology into feminism. A particularly interesting example comes from MariaLab, a Brazilian feminist association based in a squatted building in São Paulo, where debates and courses in digital skills and the politics of technology are held, and an entire room has been turned into a media and digital lab.

There are many similar organisations around the world, for example the Austrian women of Mz* Baltazar's Lab, the French women of Le Reset and their Catalan sisters from Donestech, who all pursue a twofold mission. They offer resources and mentoring to women who might be interested in creating technology, but they also map the ideas and needs of local women, putting them at the centre of all their creations. This philosophy has given rise to feminist servers like Vedetas, an independent informatics system which provides computers (specifically, those of Latino American feminist organisations) with writing and communication options other than those of mainstream social media.

As you can see, when it comes to women's creativity, the sky is the limit. Yet their efforts are grounded in one profound conviction: that technology users should not feel like economic resources to be thrown away once someone has extracted value from them. Instead, they can aspire to interact with technology as autonomous subjects, with the capacity to act and make choices, and have a clear vision of what they want from both technology and the future.

* * *

In this chapter I have relied a lot on a metaphor: Audre Lorde's image of the master's house and the master's tools. And so, before concluding, here is another allegory, much less intellectual, but well suited to our discussion.

We all know what is said of ostriches, the biggest birds on the planet: that, in the face of danger, they bury their head in the sand, hoping the threat will pass. It seems this myth started with the ancient Romans and continues to this day as we still say that those who let themselves be paralysed by life challenges are like the proverbial ostrich.

This image perfectly captures the way our society relates to patriarchy and capitalism, and the many social injustices that stem from them. Much of the time we lack the capacity to grasp such complex structures and processes. At other times we come up against them, their enormity scares us off and we abandon the challenge. We, too, bury our heads in the sand, and kid ourselves that perhaps one day we'll wake up in a world where gender injustice will have ceased to exist. Or, more simply, we pretend what's happening is not our business. And it's not necessarily our fault. We have inherited this behaviour from generations of governing elites who think in the short term and focus exclusively on contingencies, as opposed to the big picture. And we have then refined it thanks to years of cultural and political debates centred on the idea – to which I will return shortly – that radical and systemic changes are impossible and potentially harmful.

To conclude, I'd like to share a fun fact about ostriches, which I learned through a rare delve into zoology. Unlike what the myth says, when threatened, ostriches do not bury their heads in the sand. What they actually do is conceal themselves within their surroundings, or flatten their bodies on the ground. But they keep their eyes wide open and they look their enemy in the face. When their beaks are in the sand it is for one reason only: to turn over the eggs they have carefully laid, to make sure they'll open at the right time. They are taking care of the species.

I promise the metaphor is almost over, since zoology is truly not my area of expertise. I do wonder, however, whether perhaps we should start to imitate real-life ostriches, rather than those from the Roman myth? Shouldn't we look the darkest sides of the digital revolution in the eye, with a view to protecting ourselves and our communities?

For the thing is, once we have done that, just like the ostrich we'll also be able to choose between different strategies. One, as we saw, consists of seeking a provisional refuge in the many autonomous spaces stolen away from digital patriarchal capitalism: from emerging feminist social networks to feminist hacking practices. Another, perhaps even more effective, has to do with thinking carefully about where to lay our eggs, namely our ideas, with regards to different technological models, to be nourished, cherished, multiplied.

But, of course, there are many types of eggs, which I shall look at in the next chapter. Meanwhile, though, I hope to have persuaded you that sand can be used not just to disappear in, but also to build with.

CHAPTER 9

Ten ways to reform and resist

Diagnosing a problem, of course, is not the same as solving it, and envisaging a different system is much harder than dissecting the pitfalls of the one that is already standing. In my view, the alternative approaches to technology we just examined have the potential to inspire us, and to stimulate the intellectual creativity and political courage we need to drive change. But I also believe that to end the endless cycle of violence, exploitation and exclusion I have described in this book, we cannot simply rely on technological solutions. In fact, I would even say that it is the very idea of 'technical solution' that is problematic.

Evgeny Morozov, a well-respected technology scholar, has been warning us for years of the risks of what he calls 'solutionism': that is to say, the conviction that every social evil (including those triggered by technology itself) can be addressed through a quick technological fix. *Let's modify social media algorithms and online debates will all of a sudden become democratic, thoughtful and free from violence! Let's invent an ad hoc app and let's eliminate gender-based abuse from the Internet once and for all!* I am only half joking. It goes without saying that in some cases technological approaches can and should be considered. Nevertheless, it would be counterproductive and even a little dangerous to kid ourselves that technical interventions – if you like, interventions internal to the system – may replace legal reforms and, above all, political struggles.

But I don't want to overwhelm you with an endless list of policy proposals and programmes for action (plus, as my analysis has a global outlook, to which country would I address my specific policy recommendations?). As a way of compromise, I will offer ten propositions which have to do with a few macro-areas of focus: digital sector regulation, the democratisation of decision-making processes surrounding technology, the protection of tech workers' rights, and investments in digital education and support towards feminist activism. These are not meant to be exhaustive, and I ask you not to take them as recipes to be applied indiscriminately to one geographical context or another. If anything, treat them as ingredients to be variedly combined to meet specific local and national needs. As you have probably gathered, there are no magic wands. Yet there are, in my mind, choices to be made and roads to be taken, and there is much organising to be done. The rights and well-being of many depend on it. As so does our legacy for the future generations.

1 Prevent digital violence through tailored reforms and a better use of existing laws

Having started this book with stories and data about digital gender-based violence, when considering what to reform and how to resist, it seems fitting to take things from there. As I have already explained, this is a subject on which I happen to have experience in offering policy recommendations. In other words, I am rather used to being asked things like 'Do we need a brand-new law to tackle online abuse?' and 'What shall we do to regulate social media platforms' behaviour?' So here's my proverbial two cents.

In many countries, including the UK, gender-based violence laws already exist, and can be applied to online attacks. In Europe, one of the most relevant pieces of legislation is the Istanbul Convention, a specialised treaty promoted by the Council of Europe and currently ratified by more than 30 countries. However, recently there have been repeated backlashes against this type of regulation. For example, several countries that were originally part of the convention (Hungary, Turkey, Poland) have suspended its ratification process, pulled out of it, or threatened to do so. And even in countries where suitable anti-violence laws do exist, they are often disregarded in practice. Very often, there are major obstacles in the form of the judiciary and law enforcement personnel's inadequate training on matters of online abuse, and in the sexist legacy that still shapes the DNA of many legal systems. It may be that the plight of digital violence survivors is not taken seriously enough, or not as seriously as that of other abuse victims. Just think back to Tiziana Cantone and how judicial authorities failed to grasp what was happening to her, crushed as she was by a circular economy that turns women's suffering into cash.

To push for change, therefore, we must be conscious of an important difference. In some cases, criminal law reforms are needed to protect women on the Internet. In others, what's most urgent is to train relevant agencies to make the most of the legal tools we have already. For instance, a legislative intervention is necessary every time a form of digital harm is so new and unprecedented that it cannot be easily categorised within existing legal frameworks. A paradigmatic example is non-consensual pornography, a phenomenon on which legislators have rightfully started to intervene internationally. At the same time, though, let us make sure the new laws get to the heart of the matter. Many recently approved non-consensual pornography laws correctly criminalise the behaviour of individuals who share someone else's intimate photos or videos without permission. Very few, however, apply to the conduct of the platform which allowed them to share the images in the first place, or otherwise facilitated their distribution. And both you and I, by this point, know only too well what the risks are of ignoring the economic dimension of the problem.

Regulating online hate speech is a completely different story and poses different problems. The debate for and against regulation is often presented as a struggle between two fundamental and yet seemingly opposing principles: freedom of speech, and the right to be protected from incitement to hate and misogynistic (or racist, or homophobic, or, say, anti-Semitic or Islamophobic) violence. Except, from a political as well as legal standpoint, this is often a false dichotomy.

To begin with, the large majority of legal systems already admit some exceptions to free speech. And many of these exceptions (from libel to criminal threats laws) can be usefully deployed to defend women from online aggressions. On the other hand, several celebrated legal experts have been repeating for years that we also have other alternatives to choose from. One of them, well-known US law professor Danielle Citron, argues the attacks against female journalists, politicians and other Internet users could be treated as violations of existing national and international civil rights laws, such as equality acts and other bills in the areas of fair employment and non-discrimination in education and workplaces. And her reasoning is very straightforward: isn't it true that Internet violence prevents many women from using technology to learn, express themselves or do their job? Then, of course, there are countries where hate speech laws do exist, but gender is not considered to be a protected category, unlike, say, race or religion. In such cases, addressing this legal loophole has both a symbolic and a concrete, factual value for women who are victimised on the Web. (The UK is one of those countries, and MPs like Stella Creasy and Jess Phillips have long been fighting to amend hate crime laws to make them more inclusive of women's needs.[10])

10   In the UK, the digital violence landscape is likely to be affected by the Online Safety Bill, a recently revised bill that is expected to be approved by the end of 2022. Among other things, this new piece of legislation will force social media companies to 'protect children' and 'tackle illegal activities' on their platforms, and to deal with content that is not unlawful but 'harmful'. Crucially, it will also give government regulators the power to fine or prosecute platforms if they fail to do so. Both women's rights and civil rights organisations, however, have vehemently criticised the vagueness of such wording and the bill's failure to specifically designate women and other historically marginalised groups as protected categories. Other growing concerns are the absence of measures that may counterbalance the government's increased power with increased transparency commitments, and the exemption of content issued by politicians and journalists, and therefore considered 'of democratic importance', from the bill's application. In other words, there is a risk that the reform may end up policing the online behaviour of citizens without truly tackling political disinformation, algorithmic bias and the other effects that social media companies' business models have on women and other at-risk constituencies.

Overall, I'd say there are two main takeaways. First, we should make sure existing laws are fully implemented, mostly by making the law enforcement and legal professions more aware of their application to gender and of digital developments. And second, we should focus on demanding another set of legal interventions that cannot be deferred at the global level: those aimed at keeping big platforms accountable, from Facebook to Pornhub, from Google to TikTok. Which brings us straight on to proposal number two.

2 Keep platforms accountable and undermine digital monopolies

Let's immediately get one key fact out of the way. While a certain degree of freedom in experimenting with new technologies is advantageous for all, it is time to stop looking at 'innovation' (a buzzword in itself) as a process that must be kept 'free', 'unbridled' and 'disruptive'. For this view of technological progress is anything but universal or objective. The notion of commercial innovation unleashing a benign and creative destruction comes straight from one of the greatest apologists of unregulated capitalism: Austrian economist Joseph Schumpeter, voraciously read by the likes of Margaret Thatcher, Ronald Reagan and other neoliberalist politicians of the 1980s. And the point is not simply that this is a politically driven view rather than a neutral one. It is that this model hasn't served us very well over the last few decades, as is blatantly demonstrated by the stories of the many women we have encountered in these pages.

So armed with the knowledge that, every now and then, boundaries must be set around technological developments, let me start my analysis with social media platforms: spaces rife, as we know by now, with violence, marginalisation and exploitation.

Mainstream political elites, both in Europe and North America, have come to terms with the fact that regulating these platforms and even prohibiting some of their most controversial practices is neither wishful thinking nor an absurdly extreme measure. For a long time, across most continents, business practices that are unfair, unethical or harmful to workers or consumers have been subject to laws and regulation, such as fraud, workplace discrimination or misleading advertising. Why shouldn't we do the same with the behaviour of the new digital capitalists (beginning with their use of our personal data to target us based on our demographics and past choices)? Or, for instance, for decades political advertisements on TV and other traditional media have been regulated. Wouldn't it be a good and right thing to do that with online political propaganda?

Of course, Big Tech has little to gain from such reforms and, as we've seen, has long lobbied national and supranational authorities to defend its interests. But there's plenty of political arenas where these battles can be fought. See, within the EU framework, the ePrivacy Regulation, draft legislation on the protection of online communications, which for years has been the object of a constant push-pull between pro-business factions and other sectors of the European institutions more sensitive to citizens' rights to privacy. See the Digital Services Act (DSA), another EU regulatory draft currently close to implementation, which should impose tighter transparency and accountability obligations on to big platforms. In particular, they will be forced to make their moderation processes less opaque, and to submit themselves to periodical audits and controls from regulators and third parties, including NGOs or activist groups.

The advantage of this type of intervention is that, while not making platforms liable for any single piece of content posted on to them (an approach hard to put into practice), it will still push them to address the proliferation of online abuse. That said, as already pointed out by many humanitarian organisations, this is just the beginning. Both in the EU and outside, it will be necessary to translate these general guidelines into more specific directives, which may, for example, oblige platforms to remove certain content within a specific number of hours, ideally based on the seriousness of risk for the people involved. It will also be necessary to push them to pay equal attention to content published in multiple languages. And, in my view, we may need to prompt them to eliminate or review certain features of their sites, such as the algorithmic manipulation of our newsfeeds (which, according to many experts, is the main cause behind the spreading of online hate and misinformation).[11]

Plus, even undoubtedly advanced propositions such as those introduced by the DSA have their own loopholes. Specifically, during the act's negotiation in spring 2022, some clauses were expunged from the text that aimed to restrict the circulation of non-consensual pornography on adult websites, among which were porn tubes like Pornhub. Another missed opportunity has been the DSA's reluctance to intervene on data-mining business models, which, as we have learned, lie at the very heart of the matter. And let me add to this a couple of even broader considerations.

11   This is, for instance, one of the core recommendations issued by Facebook's whistle-blower Frances Haugen, who believes massive improvements could be made by organising users' social media feeds chronologically, rather than by offering them an algorithmically curated selection of contents, which favours polarisation and reinforces individual biases.

As I have repeated ad nauseam, the problem does not simply lie with a couple of big platforms or with the elite tech industry. The problem lies with an entire ecosystem, where centuries' old patriarchal oppression is intertwined with capitalistic models of production. But nobody can deny that some corporations much more than others enjoy an actual monopoly over entire digital markets, and therefore over colossal proportions of our existence. Meet Facebook/Meta, undisputed ruler of our most private conversations and intimate decisions. Meet MindGeek, master of the erotic imagination of a whole planet. Meet Google/Alphabet, which holds a monopoly over our very perception of reality, since Google's archives can nowadays be compared to a window into the world. These are all billion-dollar businesses, all private groups operating transnationally and exerting an extraordinary power over people and societies. And they are all endowed with legal structures allowing them to transcend, at least partially, national laws and jurisprudence.

This is why even though antitrust laws are not often perceived as revolutionary weapons, in this situation they can be of great use to us. In Brussels, an important step forward may happen shortly, with the final approval of yet another piece of legislation, the Digital Markets Act. In the States, on the other hand, Alexandria Ocasio-Cortez and other Democratic lawmakers are fighting a valiant battle against the new monopolies constituted by tech industry conglomerates.

Besides, I personally think that what could turn out to be equally useful are courageous taxation policies aimed at limiting the excessive powers of many tech giants, and at freeing up resources to repair some of the damage they have caused. I won't go through the details of any of these fiscal plans (as always, you'll find some relevant sources in the References), but what I will say is this: over the last few years, some proposals have been put forward in this area and they are reasonable, convincing and well thought out. Some suggest taxing income obtained through online advertisement, or by introducing AI tools that in the long term will cause job losses. Other taxation proposals focus on income derived from commercial services offered via retail platforms. And in some countries, similar ideas are already being tested. Even more importantly, discussions are taking place to decide how to redistribute these taxes. Which, just to mention one of the many possibilities, may include reinforcing sources of democratic information and programmes to prevent online hate and misinformation. Or redistributive interventions tailored to guarantee more equal access to technology regardless of differences based on class, race, geography and, obviously, gender. I don't know about you, but I can no longer stomach the sight of little girls on a pavement trying to connect to the Wi-Fi of a fast-food outlet to do their homework, while a short drive away tech businesses make millions daily.

3 Regulate algorithmic developments and make them more transparent

There is another area of regulation where we can no longer procrastinate and that is the design, use and commercialisation of AI techniques. These days too many key decisions depend on algorithmic systems for us to allow the functioning of algorithms themselves to remain like a black box: opaque, mysterious, potentially distorted by sexist, racist and classist biases. In this field, too, we are lucky enough to be able to build upon a few compelling, comprehensive policy proposals, many of which were put together by women we have already met (computer scientists Timnit Gebru and Joy Buolamwini, and engineer and former Meta employee Frances Haugen). For several years, and in collaboration with other AI experts, women like Timnit, Joy and Frances have requested that procedures to appeal the outcomes of algorithmic decisions are introduced. And that could make a difference.

I presume you have not forgotten the Black women who had their mortgage applications denied, the queer women who were discriminated against on the job, and all because of processes shaped by algorithmic prejudices. So, if the organisations that use AI tools to make sensitive choices and allocate crucial resources were forced to equip themselves with such appeal mechanisms, all of these people could signpost the discriminations they suffered and ask for rectification or compensation. Several other options would also be relatively easy to introduce. One is the creation of ad hoc independent structures whose task would be the auditing of the algorithms used by both governments and private companies. Imagine, in practice, a sort of 'Algorithm Independent Authority', accountable not to executive agencies but to citizens, and which individuals, organisations and communities could refer to, including to obtain information on specific algorithms' functioning. Wouldn't that be at least a useful point of departure?

Another idea that, in my opinion, we should push forward decisively is that of an international moratorium on the use of specific forms of AI (say, facial-recognition software) in certain sensitive operations, such as those carried out by the police and the military.

At the end of the day, the question is rather simple: because a given technology enabled us to do something we couldn't do yesterday, should we necessarily conclude it is always worth doing it today, regardless of the social impact? To go back to a case we discussed already in depth: do you think we truly need software that based on an image allows us to deduce whether the person portrayed is a woman, or perhaps a trans woman or a lesbian? Who benefits from this? At the moment, I can tell you that the applications of automatic gender-recognition tools have mostly been electronic advertisement banners showing differentiated ads to women and men, and girls-only entertainment apps. Is it worth it? Is it sensible to leave surveillance agencies and other powerful actors experimenting with these techniques, knowing they might help them profile women or LGBTQ+ populations?

Personally, going back to the notion of setting boundaries, I find it rather obvious that some restrictions should be set up. And not out of a Luddite mentality based on 'banning evil and dystopian algorithms', or from a desire to return to a rose-tinted time that never existed in reality. But some boundaries and rules should be drawn with a view to investing the time, resources and funding for the development of tools that might actually benefit and assist people and communities. And to put technology where it should be: at the service of human beings, rather than in obscure corridors of power where it has remained for too long.

4 Democratise the organisations where key decisions around technology are made

I have talked many times in this book about circular problems. And many times I found it was like a snake biting its own tail. I am sure you won't be surprised, then, if after having listed the many policy decisions still to be made I want to consider the ways in which they can be made more inclusively and fairly.

We already know that people involved in the decision-making processes surrounding technology – within the tech industry, in governments and across other regulatory bodies – should be both diverse and sensitive to social and ethical concerns. Nevertheless, while diversity and fair representation are certainly necessary, they are not sufficient. Paradoxically, reducing the great collective political struggle for gender (or racial, or social) justice to the individualistic mantra of 'diversity' within organisations might even produce the opposite effect. The risk is that historically exclusionary employers and political institutions will try to clean up their image by welcoming into their ranks a couple of women, people of colour or LGBTQ+ individuals, while actually taking no further action or making any meaningful change.

Nor is it forward-thinking or even legitimate or fair to burden individual women or any individual with the responsibility of building collective change. Some of them might not have a progressive agenda on digital issues. Others might not have the energy to fight solitary battles or might find themselves in a weak position within their respective organisations. So gender quotas, women's networks, specialised subsidies and financial support programmes to boost the presence of women and racial and sexual minorities in tech, politics and other workplaces are all very well but these measures must be strengthened and expanded by applying the recommendations on participatory decision-making and design techniques discussed in Chapter 8. Techniques grounded, as you may remember, in the idea that diversity and equal representation are only a starting point.

That is to say, individuals, their identities and their experiences do, obviously, matter. But what matters perhaps even more are the structures, methods and organisational cultures that facilitate or constrain their actions. Therefore, to develop better technologies and tech policies, we need to build different organisations. Organisations that at every step (from the initial conception of a tool or policy decision, up to the last phases of testing, implementation and monitoring) take into account questions like: What are the effects of these actions on women and other historically oppressed groups, and on communities and territories? How do we know this? Who did we talk and listen to, who got a seat at the table, and which voices have been included in the conversation?

And it is worthy of note that it is not only the field of feminist design that offers precious insights and good practices. In the field of organisational policy-making, for example, people have been talking for years of 'gender mainstreaming', namely a methodology to integrate a gender perspective within administrative procedures. Cities such as Vienna and Barcelona have created whole city council bodies devoted to such strategies. There is fertile ground to grow from waiting for us outside. It is up to us, as citizens, residents and consumers, to demand that it is used well. I will come back to the potential and pitfalls of consumer-led activism, but before doing that there are a couple of points that must be urgently spelled out.

5 Take workplace sexual harassment and the digital gender gap seriously

Let me say it again, to avoid any misunderstanding: when I talk of democratising decision-making in technology, or, more generally, in politics and policies, we face two gargantuan barriers.

The first is sexual harassment at work and in the public space.

It remains a formidable instrument to control and silence women, and to undermine their claims and their struggles. I'm sure you remember well the stories of the many female tech workers we met in previous chapters, all harassed or discriminated against as they tried to do their job, and perhaps remedy some of the many negative externalities of the digital revolution. And I presume you'll agree with me that this is yet another of those areas where it is hard to break the vicious circle. Violence and discrimination in the workplace weaken women's voices in the debates and activities concerning technology. Their needs are constantly pushed towards the margins. Their marginalisation translates into the creation of exclusionary technology and the tech industry's frustrating inertia regarding matters of sexism and abuse. Consequently, there are a few things that need to be done now.

Workplaces and political and decision-making arenas (from tech companies to governments, from other firms within the tech industry supply chain to political parties) must all establish rapid, safe and effective mechanisms for reporting and managing sexual harassment complaints. Serious prevention programmes must be put in place at the organisational and societal level. And there are no more valid excuses not to build, sustain and fund women's professional support networks and, above all, organisations dedicated to assisting victimised women and their communities.

The other issue we can no longer brush under the carpet is the digital gender gap, which afflicts the entire world, whose influence on women's comparatively scarce involvement in the construction of a more inclusive digital future need not be further explained. How can any decisions made on technology matters be fair if millions of women and girls do not even have access to the Internet? How can we hope to make technology design and regulation more just and participatory if a substantial number of the world's population is consistently less likely to know how technology works, and is unable to familiarise itself with it? We have already seen how different, intricate factors correspond to the digital gender divide: the still relatively high costs of many devices, the lack of Internet connection in large areas of the world and the absence of serious plans to tackle obscene economic inequalities. I first refer you to some of the big-picture considerations I discussed in Chapter 8. And then I dare you to re-emphasise a rather self-evident truth: even in this area, the tech tax propositions and the redistributive interventions I mentioned previously would certainly be a good place to start – especially if combined with efforts to undermine existing stereotypes on the relationship between gender and technology and to support groups typically excluded from digital access. I am thinking of scholarship programmes and code camps for women interested in STEM subjects, such as those currently being tested in some countries of the Global South, and digital training projects targeting elderly or disabled women, centred on their own interests and needs. Lesbians Who Tech, a global community of queer technologists, have put forward an intriguing model which, among its various activities, funds coding diplomas for LBT women and non-binary people.

I am not citing these specific examples as an Olympics of the politically correct, based on the need to demonstrate that I have not forgotten anyone. It is because, as I hope to have clearly shown by now, different forms of marginalisation truly reinforce one another, and then get inscribed into our technologies. Therefore, to protect and empower everyone, the fight for digital justice really cannot leave anyone behind. Which takes me to the next points.

6 Recognise and defend tech workers' rights at all levels

We are living in an age where protections, guarantees and even basic principles in defence of workers' rights are under constant attack. Yet as soon as you start discussing the conditions in which some of the most vulnerable women within the tech industry are forced to operate, it stirs up a wasps' nest. *It's the global economy, baby. Workers deserve our solidarity, yes, but what can we do? If we enhance their protections, firms will outsource their activities elsewhere.* Or even: *How can it be our fault if other countries have very weak labour laws?* Let me be clear: complexities related to economic globalisation do undoubtedly exist and have painful consequences. But a civilisation worthy of its name has the duty to examine those complexities and prevent them from crushing human rights so that a smartphone may be built or a digital app may function, especially considering that workers around the world have very clear ideas on the steps we could take to do so.

For example, some of these ideas have recently been presented by Isabella Plunkett, the social media content moderator we met in Chapter 1. Together with a lawyer specialising in digital work, Cori Crider, she has spoken to an Irish parliamentary committee about a few concrete ways to regulate the moderation sector. Among other suggestions, Isabella and Cori advised outlawing non-disclosure and other confidentiality agreements that are increasingly spreading across the tech industry which prevent workers from speaking up about their conditions. This view can be connected to a legal principle entrenched in the legislation of many countries: the notion that private firms have a duty of care towards their employees and other stakeholders.

Without a doubt, and especially in ever-evolving fields like technology, duty of care may sound very vague and needs to be specified and translated into more concrete regulations. However, in the case of social media content moderators, it is easy to see how this framework could be leveraged and used to prohibit excessively long, debilitating shift patterns and to oblige platform companies to provide moderators with professional medical assistance.

As we know, many complications derive from multinational tech companies' tendency to delegate part of their operations to intermediary companies. And yes, it is true that by regulating their behaviour it risks endangering the jobs of already fragile workforces outside the West. Still, a partial solution is before our eyes and consists of pushing platforms to keep in-house the activities linked to their core business (content moderation among these), so as to avoid creating first- and second-class work categories. And to do so using both the carrot and the stick.

Another problem, which I touched upon when talking about gig work and the influencer economy, is that tech workers are often deprived of collective instruments to negotiate with their employers. One of the ways in which this happens is through their classification as 'freelancers', 'partners' and other imprecise terms (you'll remember the strike of Seema Singh and her brave Indian colleagues). However, legal experts and gig workers' associations have envisaged a few areas of intervention. A first possibility would be to establish specific legal protection for gig workers willing to sue a platform regarding the categorisation of their employment status. A second one has to do with shifting the burden of proof from the worker to the platforms (in other words, forcing them to prove that their employees enjoy such flexible working conditions as to be classified as freelance). And a third idea is to prohibit (or at least to carefully regulate) algorithmic mechanisms of the allocation of work shifts, which on many apps end up penalising women gig workers.

Yet another useful measure could be to introduce tax incentives and other support strategies to encourage the rise of cooperative platforms and other democratic forms of digital gig work, where both the earnings and the platforms themselves would be collectively owned and managed by the workers, notwithstanding the importance of the recommendations summarised in the next point.

7 Support new unions and other forms of organising

Social media content moderators in various countries were denied permission to constitute internal unions. My friend Hannah Jewell, a journalist and former content writer for BuzzFeed, reported in her book *We Need Snowflakes* (2022) the challenges she and her colleagues faced when trying to get a union recognised by senior management in the UK. And Google, according to more than one testimony, made life very hard for a group of employees (many of whom were involved in the famous women's walkout of 2018) who tried to create an association of the same kind. The lords of tech do not like unions and it is not hard to see why.

Yet the *sine qua non* to protect women in technology (and any tech worker, regardless of gender) is to recognise their right to unionise and to reinforce the bodies that represent them, which, undoubtedly, need to keep up with the times: in some cases new unions are needed, more specialised, or more democratic and more in tune with the new forms of work and exploitation generated by the digital revolution. In others, where freedom of association and labour rights are undermined by local legislation or organisational culture, other forms of self-organisation can also be considered, from class actions to obtain damage compensation, to coordinated actions alongside NGOs supporting whistle-blowers, to employees who need to report their employers.

Altogether, though, we must not make the mistake of considering unions obsolete instruments inadequate for the digital era. Plus, within the tech industry unions are blooming everywhere and to see this you only have to check out websites such as Tech Workers Coalition (TWC) and Coworker.org.

TWC is an international coalition uniting tech workers from several countries, alongside individuals with expertise in community organisation. Starting in 2014, TWC has assisted and connected the most heterogenous types of tech professionals: from digital content producers to riders, from designers to gig drivers. On its portal, the network also includes an up-to-date list of national unions active in all of these areas.

A look at Coworker.org, on the other hand, may give you a glimpse of the ways in which we can all contribute to tech workers' ongoing efforts. Launched – as it happens – by two women, trade unionist Michelle Miller and social entrepreneur and digital expert Jess Kutch, the platform makes a myriad of resources available to tech workforces. On the site, you'll find information on rights, articles demystifying complex labour legislation and advice on how to organise in the workplace. And you'll find petitions and crowdfunding appeals started by workers across the world. Among these are feminist battles: for more adequate parental leave for Netflix employees; and an international campaign started by emerging union Gig Workers Rising, which is currently asking Uber, Lyft and other driving apps to modify their deactivation policies, so as to empower drivers against the murky, at times unfair, decisions made by platforms' algorithms.

In a nutshell, technology production processes take place on a global scale and there is evidence that workers pay a price for it. But, as demonstrated by TWC, Coworker.org and other analogous organisations, workers' solidarity is also going global, as is the popular support for their efforts.

8 Demand cleaner supply chains

Now we have come to an extraordinarily thorny problem: that of the multinational tech industry supply chains. I say 'thorny' due to a long list of reasons. First of all, it is very hard to regulate activities, both productive and extractive, that cross a number of countries. A second key issue is that even when legislators attempt in good faith to prevent tech companies from causing or facilitating human rights violations, vulnerable communities are unfairly caught in the middle. I hinted at this risk when discussing the international legislation on conflict minerals and its unintentional effects: boycotting a given resource, firm or business practice may, for example, hit an innocent local population heavily.

The argument I made earlier, though, still applies: such valid and legitimate concerns cannot be used as an excuse to stick with the status quo. Because at least two things are as plain as day. First, tech companies and the wider economic systems gravitating around them have the obligation to monitor, prevent and mitigate human and social risks across their entire supply chain (an obligation covering the safety of women who extract the raw materials used to build our gadgets, as well as those who assemble them). Second, national and international authorities have the duty to make sure such obligations are enforced, and transgressors punished.

Many of the previous points I have raised in this chapter are also relevant. No real monitoring of tech supply chains is possible without questioning the impact of tech production on women and girls, as it isn't possible to prevent or remedy existing violations without starting from women's and workers' self-organising efforts.

But we should also acknowledge that we, too, as a civil society, have some weapons in our arsenal. One of these, so-called ethical consumption, has in the past pushed several corporations to adopt less questionable practices and led to the emergence of 'cleaner' products. Proof of this is the fact that, for many of us, drinking Fairtrade coffee or buying fruit and veg from local producers has become a daily habit: we can find the coffee at our local café and the groceries at the farmers' market. Yet, as you may have noticed, 'ethical' smartphones and laptops are harder to come by. This is partially because our devices are made up of so many components that it is difficult to carefully certify their origin. On the other hand, it is also true that the tech industry has so far been exposed to less pressure than, say, the food sector, or the diamond or fast fashion industries. As a result (with the exception of isolated peaks of media attention following episodes such as the Foxconn suicides), many Big Tech businesses have little incentive to propose gadgets less smeared with sweat and blood.

Finally, the use of ethical shopping as an advocacy strategy has yet another limitation. When conveying the message that we, as consumers, have the ability and duty to prevent workers' exploitation, we risk encouraging cynical companies and sluggish regulators to relinquish their responsibilities. But while we shouldn't burden ourselves with someone else's charges, neither should we make the opposite mistake and forget that, when consuming and buying, we should be able to rely on certain rights and on a certain degree of power. So no, our solidarity and activism must not become an excuse to depict a huge political and systemic problem as a matter of mere individual behavioural change. Yet there are very good reasons to test this power of ours and flex our muscles, even when it comes to our high-tech shopping choices.

9 Educate ourselves and others on technology and on gender

I chose to devote my life to research, activism and teaching, so it probably won't surprise you that my last reflections pertain to the need to educate ourselves and others, to build and exchange knowledge and to support feminist activism.

And I'd like to add that there is truly nothing trivial about any of these goals. In fact, I do not feel I am being an alarmist when I say that we all have to defend ourselves from the oppressive mechanisms of patriarchal digital capitalism, many of which affect us from dangerously close. I believe that to get ourselves out of the morass, education is one of the most powerful self-defence tactics that has ever existed.

At least two types of intervention, then, can no longer be delayed. One concerns digital education, meant in a much broader sense than what most schools and governments seem to have provided so far. It is certainly useful to offer people training to acquire digital skills that may help them study, work, find jobs and make their life a little easier. But it is equally important to help societies develop a more comprehensive outlook on the forces that hide behind technology. In other words, we need public information campaigns on digital rights and digital ethics, and *we need them now*. As we need school and university curricula that integrate content on the politics and ethics of technology, as well as specialised adult training for workplaces on the very same topics. And to carry out all this, in time it will be necessary to continue allocating funds to research in this area and to the translation of this knowledge into accessible and less specialist language.

And there is also a second, timely educational investment that is needed. Still today, in too many parts of the world (including in the West), millions of children and teenagers are deprived of their right to be educated on issues of gender, sexuality and healthy relationships, and to learn how to interact with one another in a free, egalitarian and mutually respectful manner. The immense damage caused by this is there for everyone to see. How can we possibly imagine that online interactions may one day become more civil and less sexist and violent if the prevention of gender-based violence is not part of our educational background? How can we hope to see progress in women's rights in the workplace if we never teach younger generations about the gendered issues of work (or of any other aspect of human life)?

Besides, over the last few years, it is hard to ignore how sex education has become a bargaining chip for many unscrupulous politicians internationally, who have transformed the topic into a political hot potato. *Down with 'gender theory' schools! Let's protect our children from 'gay propaganda' and 'feminazis'! Gender education is brainwashing and sexualising our kids and destroys the foundations of our society!*

The tragedy is that, by means of such twisted lies, some reactionary political forces across the world have gained the loyalty of religious groups and parents' associations. And, in so doing, they have disseminated chaos, consolidated alliances and gained more votes. Meanwhile, very few progressive parties have had the foresight to turn the battle for meaningful and pertinent sex and relationship education into a priority. I, however, am convinced that such a battle should be fought urgently, in the interest of girls and of all children regardless of gender, who deserve holistic, intersectional school teaching, sensitive to issues of sexual consent and, of course, to the complexities of online exchanges. And if we don't take to the barricades for this right of theirs, what else should we really do it for?

10 One, ten, a hundred, a thousand feminist struggles

You have probably noticed that in this chapter I have alternated recommendations meant for political institutions, the private sector, individuals and communities. I have done this in full awareness that such levels of action are different from one another and that an individual consumer hardly has the same degree of influence or agency as a corporation or a national regulator. But I have deemed it important to reflect on how such various levels of action are connected to one another. Indeed, as I have already tried to explain (say, when talking about our power as workers, consumers or members of a polity), I am convinced we should put an end to harmful and artificial distinctions between 'those who decide' and 'those who must put up with the decisions'.

Just consider the way we talk of lawmakers, often treating them as a sort of *deus ex machina*, who, benevolently, every now and then deign to give us a law or recognise a right of ours. In reality, we owe all the great progressive legislation of the last century to political battles started on the ground (and the same could be said for any significant progress in terms of workplace democracy). In brief, it is within the human capability to organise that lies the potential to change our societies for the better. And it is mostly on that capability that we should rely in these troubled times of digital transition.

So please allow me to conclude on a not particularly objective note, since I am myself involved in the movements whose praises I am about to sing. Because, you see, I believe that an especially extraordinary potential is to be found in the rich tradition of women's organising and, of course, of feminist thought, without taking anything away from other great historical social science movements, with which feminists must build bridges and coalitions.

Yet I find it undeniable that very few organisational phenomena in contemporary history have demonstrated an intellectual and political vibrancy comparable to those of women's movements and have been equally successful in bringing about rapid and profound change. For this exact reason, I am persuaded that everybody gains from intense involvement in feminist debates and struggles surrounding technology and digital capitalism, at the local, national and international level.

At the same time, as I already noted, feminism and feminists still badly need allies. And not just because in order to disrupt the many vicious circles activated by digital capitalism, women's demands and needs can be usefully voiced and defended alongside those of other social groups, but also because we presently find ourselves at a crucial crossroads.

Today, in so many ways, the language of gender justice is considered 'fashionable' and finds more space in public debates than it did a few years ago. This offers us a formidable window of opportunity, which we will take advantage of. But there are also some potential dangers. The first concerns so-called pinkwashing, of which I spoke already. A victim of its very success, feminism has at times been appropriated, depoliticised and diluted to the point of losing its force. And we must be on guard to prevent this from happening again. Another risk, completely opposed to the first one, has to do with the misogynistic backlashes that often follow feminist movements' achievements and successes. I have talked about this when examining the political platforms of many populist and nationalist leaders, whether it is Jair Bolsonaro or Donald Trump or Vladimir Putin, Mohammed bin Salman or Viktor Orbán, Alexander Lukashenko or Matteo Salvini, in many countries a new, organised opposition has risen against feminist values and has sometimes translated into heavy crackdowns on women's rights. Amid such a difficult time, I cannot help but conclude with both an invitation and a call to arms: an *invitation* to join all feminist organisations and efforts you meet along the way; and a *call* to support them and to accompany them in the search for answers to the many questions we are still grappling with, out of a spirit of justice and solidarity, but also to be on the right side of history.

CONCLUSIONS

In defence of (feminist) utopias

A while ago one of my Cambridge master's students (a smart, thoughtful, passionate young woman) asked me if I deemed systemic transformations to be possible. We were talking, unsurprisingly, of the intersections between patriarchy, capitalism and technology. She was telling me of how desperately angry she often feels and of how badly she needs to redirect that anger towards the construction of a different future, for women and for all. It's just that to her, the future to be built seems so far away that she struggles to imagine a concrete road towards it.

I admit it wasn't difficult for me to recognise myself in her words. My student is not much younger than me and we both went to school in the West in the 1990s and 2000s. This means for decades we have both been absorbing three messages that have considerable implications. One: we were told we were born in the best of all possible worlds. Which means that even when things don't work out, we were warned, we should hold on to the system as it is, for there were no alternatives bar catastrophe and doom.

After all, the Berlin Wall had just fallen and many political and economic experiments started before we were born seemed to have run their course. It was fashionable to argue that 'history had ended' and that no other way to organise society was realistic or desirable. Those who disagreed were considered lunatics who didn't do politics but utopian daydreaming.

Two: millennial girls like ourselves (or at least Western ones) were taught we really have nothing to complain about. Don't we enjoy full human rights, both legally and factually? The occasional rape or femicide, of course, did end up in the papers, but we got reassured that was due to a few rotten apples – isolated monsters in a solidly post-patriarchal world, or that they were from 'backward' cultures, 'less advanced' than ours.

For that matter, it wasn't only gender-based violence which was reduced to an individual problem: that era's whole mantra took the individual as a measure of all things. Concepts seeking to capture the structural functioning of society (patriarchy or capitalism, anyone?) were regarded as obsolete, inadequate to explain contemporary developments.

Three: during our childhood tech gadgets of all sorts were beginning to sprout like mushrooms and our generation was told that technology would make this already luminous present even better. Youth unemployment rising alarmingly? Fear not: the digital revolution will create new jobs. Oft-ignored climate scientists warning us of the dangers of global warming? 'Clean' technologies will reverse it. We were even invited not to worry about the increasing atomisation of society: the Internet will unite humanity, turning the world into an idyllic global village. What marvellous times to grow up and be alive.

Except that year after year, this orgy of arrogance was gradually replaced by the frustrations of millions of former children (above all, of former little girls), left to cope with the bitter taste of broken promises. And these disappointments were not felt by my generation alone. Our parents, grandparents and younger siblings were all left in the cold, one after the other. First came the financial crisis of 2007–08. Then the great recession of 2008–09. Then more global economic shocks. Social and economic inequalities rose dramatically. Digital capitalism progressively showed its true face and its sexist traits became so evident that even the post-patriarchy myth soon lost its power.

Should it come as a surprise that my student feels at times as though her back is being pushed against the wall? Although she has long stopped believing in the fairy tales she was fed as a child, she struggles to see a way out of this. Raise your hand if you have never felt like she does. For years we have all been subjected to a potent indoctrination and so we find ourselves without the capacity to believe in radical change and to imagine a day different from the present one. The mental muscle we need to picture a paradigm shift, that exquisite flexibility of the heart and the mind, feels blocked, feels atrophied.

So, we may well be intrigued by the suggestions of 'feminist technology' and reform propositions but we are thoroughly unable to contextualise them in a bigger picture of change towards which *we* should be working. I am using the word *we* for a reason, because most of the time I also feel that my muscle is atrophied. I remain convinced, however, that exercising it might be the single most useful thing we can do in the present moment, even more than carrying out all the other interventions and practices we have considered so far to remedy the injustices triggered by the digital revolution.

I'd like to keep you a little longer, as I attempt to address the fundamental questions asked by my student. As well as to persuade you that, yes, our political imagination muscle might be barely functioning due to the long inertia, but it is still there and is really worth using.

* * *

During the last ten years, I first studied and then taught at the University of Cambridge: an institution where women like myself (and my student mentioned above) had not been fully admitted until 1948. This detail is highly relevant to our analysis, which is why I hope you'll allow me this last, brief digression.

You should know that when, over a century ago, courageous women activists fought for their right to graduate within the university, male students and professors waged a war against them. They insulted them in newspapers; they took to the streets as an act of protest and symbolically hung the image of a female student from a university building. In 1921, they even attacked in force a women-only college. The principal, a veteran feminist and suffrage fighter, had the gates locked just in time. About 1,400 men showed up to try to break them, with (male) police officers standing by and watching. The women who dared to expect to learn and exchange knowledge had to be punished to protect the status quo. They were dangerous fools, subversive utopians.

Those of you who are familiar with the history of women's

movements will probably know how recurrent these insults are across the centuries. More or less at the same time, for example, they were addressed against the suffragettes: another bunch of undefeatable warriors, who, for the sake of fighting for women to have the right to vote, accepted imprisonment and tolerated savage beatings and force-feeding when on hunger strike. The 'dangerous utopian' mark of shame was also used against activists in the 1960s, who strived for another inalienable woman's right: that of bodily autonomy and choosing whether or not to continue a pregnancy. A right – it is worth remembering – that is still under attack in many countries. And there are more. Throughout history, Black and Brown women who spoke up about how it felt to be experiencing a double form of oppression have also been called 'madwomen', 'dangerous utopians'. So have the female factory workers, farmers, trade unionists and strikers who, over the last 150 years, screamed to anyone listening that women are exploited even more than men.

Paradoxically, however, all these labels, chosen to be vulgarly offensive, were indeed striking a chord. Because it is profoundly, fabulously true that those extraordinary women had the enviable ability to imagine something that wasn't there: a revolutionary transformation starting from the margins (namely from the silenced voices of women) to disrupt intersecting injustices, in the interest of the many. This is an ability that in itself is something radical, something dangerous and something subversive, in the best possible way. It might even be said that it often goes hand in hand with a streak of madness: the holy madness of artists, poets, freedom warriors, of all those who could picture in their dreams a very different reality.

The assumption that these feminist pioneers' outlook on life was abstract rather than concrete, grounded in fantasy rather than reality, was a huge misunderstanding. All the great feminist revolutions (to be precise, all the great social struggles in human history) have been characterised by a constant dialectic between ideas and actions, between dreams of change and strategic analysis stemming from political militancy. For this very reason, the imaginative visions of the feminists of ages past have become through time historical fact, empirical evidence, widely accepted reality.

That said, it is clear that without the political imagination muscle I mentioned above very little could have been strategised, obtained, let alone revolutionised. So why not rename that muscle *utopia muscle*, if for no other reason than out of respect for those who have been called that word as an insult? And why not tap into the rich heritage of their luminous ideas and struggles every time we feel that that muscle is truly stuck?

It is those feminists of the past that my student and I ended up talking about during our exchange. To be more specific, I reminded that young woman, filled with love and rightful rage, that it was thanks to those sisters, often disbelieved, often insulted, and to their courage to conceive enormous transformations that she and I have the chance to talk to one another today. She a student, I a teacher, in a university whose doors have been opened for us as a result of utopian fights. She and I are both free to vote, to control our reproductive life, to sue those who discriminate against us in the workplace; yet we are both well aware that none of this is enough, and that we *can* and *must* ask for more.

For, obviously, utopias never directly translate into an Eden or an Atlantis. Utopias, by definition, push us a step forward, towards an alternative to injustice and dominion that always exists potentially and yet must be built by questioning the political nuances of the present.

It mustn't be forgotten that some of the historical feminist movements' crowning achievements are themselves in danger, or at least under attack. Just think of abortion rights, largely disregarded in many countries and the constitutional right to an abortion taken away in the United States in 2022. Other rights (such as the right to education and parity at work) are enjoyed by some women but not others (usually based on class, racial, geographical or sexual identity differences), and need to be extended and reinforced.

That said, we must not forget that what women have already achieved offers plenty of evidence that structural changes are possible, as far as someone is able to conceive them and that utopia is a collective and not an individual activity.

Towards the end of our conversation, I also told my student that several utopian views (and I mean this in the best, most concrete sense of the term) are already on the table. They have risen amid our decades of cynical and individualistic indoctrination and concern the very topics we have been discussing in this book. I will mention a few of them as a way of conclusion, although very briefly and without the in-depth analysis they deserve (as usual, though, you'll find some sources in the References).

I'd like to mention, first of all, the reasonings and the proposals centred around the notion of the Internet as a universal human right. Should this principle be institutionalised, it would trigger a substantial domino effect. Local and national political institutions, for example, would be forced to implement that right through public interventions and, whenever necessary, redistributive policies. Incidentally, they should also commit themselves, once and for all, to eliminating the obscene digital gender gap we have often talked about.

A second, equally powerful, vision concerns the conceptualisation of data extracted from online interactions as a 'common'. The vision has been interpreted rather differently across time and space, but the principle behind it is simple. In the case of our data, the idea is to have it harvested not by private, profit-driven companies but by social, community-owned platforms, and to use it for social research and for developing tools such as better transportation and healthcare practices, including services targeting women and other under-served categories. Can you imagine the radical, life-changing potential of such a shift?

A third, seemingly visionary and yet totally feasible, proposition (already pushed forward by many social movements and successfully experimented with at the micro-territorial level) concerns the introduction of a universal basic income. Creating a social safety net would empower the most vulnerable women within the tech supply chain (as well as millions of other people) to free themselves from exploitation and to negotiate better working conditions. A universal basic income, among other things, would also have specific advantages in terms of reallocation of care work between the genders – a problem I have often touched upon in this book. I do not mean that with a guaranteed family income it should be women that give up paid work. What I am suggesting is that increased economic safety might help households and, indeed, entire communities reach a better balance between work and family life, and experiment with shared care practices. I am obviously simplifying to the extreme complex and nuanced debates, but there is no doubt that here we are talking of the feminist revolution in a nutshell: turning work from being a necessity of life that leads straight into exploitation into a choice and a right.

We have talked of how some of capitalism's and patriarchy's worst aspects are often entrenched in the functioning of our organisations, and of private firms specifically. Yet this does not mean it might not be possible to design different organisational and economic models. I have already referred to several examples of cooperative platforms, co-managed by the workforce. To these, we must add other models of social enterprises, which subordinate profit to social purposes, and which offer further inspiration and food for thought. And we must add other, more wide-ranging visions, which consider national reforms of business laws and aim to subvert the model that currently affords enormous power to investors and leaves them free to prioritise profit over human, social and environmental sustainability. Nor do we lack conceptual efforts, many of which are coming from indigenous and Global South feminists, aimed at rethinking the management of natural and digital resources (among them the minerals involved in technology production). Here, too, the idea is to democratise such operations, entrusting them not to the private sector but to local populations.

As you can see, despite the heterogeneity of such approaches, we are talking of ideas which are at once realistic and malleable enough to be tested and pursued through the course of our lifetime, and sufficiently powerful and imaginative to rock the boat and initiate substantial change. It goes without saying that a feminist utopia embodying a definite alternative to the current incarnations of patriarchy and capitalism is yet to come. Still, we have got plenty of ideas and these can be pursued with contingent political strategies and the inspiration we draw from past feminist struggles.

More than anything, it seems to me that the very existence of these approaches and these visions demonstrates something crucial and worth celebrating: namely, that our utopia muscle is still there, ready to be exercised; to be used to smash current harmful paradigms and to act as guidance and as a talisman in times to come. And, believe me, nobody can take that away from us.

REFERENCES

Introduction and author's note

—*On the night . . . suicide*: On Carolina Picchio's story:

- Kington, T., 2013. 'Facebook challenge after girl's suicide over insults', *Sydney Morning Herald*, 28/05. https://www.smh.com.au/technology/facebook-challenge-after-girls-suicide-over-insults-20130528-2n804.html

—*On the 17th . . . average'*: On Tian Yu's case and the suicides at Foxconn:

- Chan, J., 2013. 'A suicide survivor: the life of a Chinese worker', *New Technology, Work and Employment*, 18/07, 28(2) 84–99. doi: 10.1111/ntwe.12007
- Ha, P., 2010. 'Foxconn Suicides: Eh, They're "Below Average", says Apple CEO', *Time*, 01/06. https://techland.time.com/2010/06/01/foxconn-suicides-eh-theyre-below-average

—*I have . . . geography*: On the notion of intersectionality:

- Crenshaw, K.W., 2017. *On Intersectionality: Essential Writings*, The New Press.

—*At the same time . . . may be*: Here the reference list would be rather long. I recommend, in particular:

- Arruzza, C., Bhattacharya, T., Fraser, N., 2019. *Feminism for the 99%. A Manifesto*, Verso.
- hooks, b., 1984. *Feminist Theory: from margin to center*, South End Press.

—*In this book . . . techniques*: As a way of introduction to the relationships between patriarchy and capitalism, as well as to the concept of 'logic', I recommend:

- Acker, J., 2004. 'Gender, Capitalism and Globalization', *Critical Sociology*, 30(1), 17–41. doi: 10.1163/156916304322981668
- Thornton, P.H. and Ocasio, W., 2008. 'Institutional Logics', *The SAGE Handbook of Organizational Institutionalism*, 840, 99–128.
- Wajcman, J., 2006. 'TechnoCapitalism Meets TechnoFeminism: Women and Technology in a Wireless World', *Labour & Industry: a journal of the social and economic relations of work*, 16(3) 7–20. doi: 10.1080/10301763.2006.10669327

Chapter 1

—*Not that long . . . platforms:* On Jess Phillips's story:

- Asthana, A., 2016. 'Labour MP Jess Phillips installing "panic room" at office following threats', *Guardian*, 16/08. https://www.theguardian.com/politics/2016/aug/16/labour-mp-jess-phillips-installing-panic-room-at-office-following-threats
- Phillips, J., 2018. *Everywoman: One Woman's Truth About Speaking the Truth*, Penguin.

—*Let's start . . . uploads*: Here are the details of the studies I mention:

* Amnesty International, 2018. *Troll Patrol Findings*. https://decoders.amnesty.org/projects/troll-patrol/findings
* Di Stefano, M. and Al-Othman, H., 2019. 'UKIP Candidate Carl Benjamin Has Talked Again About Raping Labour MP Jess Phillips And Now She Wants Action', BuzzFeed, 03/05. https://www.buzzfeed.com/markdistefano/jess-phillips-carl-benjamin-new-rape-comments
* Knight, S., 2019. 'Facebook reportedly receives half a million revenge porn complaints each month', *TechSpot*, 18/11. https://www.techspot.com/news/82816-facebook-reportedly-receives-half-million-revenge-porn-complaints.html
* Phifer, D., 2019. 'Alexandria Ocasio-Cortez Responds To Video Calling Her An "Enemy Of Freedom"', *Newsweek*, 28/05. https://www.newsweek.com/alexandria-ocasio-cortez-responds-video-calling-her-enemy-freedom-messages-1437681
* Plan International, 2020. *Free to Be Online?*. https://plan-international.org/publications/free-to-be-online/
* Statista Research Department, 2022. *Facebook: number of monthly active users worldwide 2008–2022*. https://www.statista.com/statistics/264810/number-of-monthly-active-facebook-users-worldwide
* Wells, M. and Mitchell, K.J., 2014. 'Patterns of Internet Use and Risk of Online Victimization for Youth With and Without Disabilities', *Journal of Special Education*, 48(3) 204–13. doi: 10.1177/0022466913479141

—*According to recent . . . job*: My source here is:

* *The Economist*, Intelligence Unit, 2021. 'Measuring the

prevalence of online violence against women'. https://
onlineviolencewomen.eiu.com

—During her workday, Isabella . . . worldwide: On Isabella's testimony:

- Criddle, C., 2021. 'Facebook moderator: "Every day was a
  nightmare"', BBC News, 12/05. https://www.bbc.co.uk/
  news/technology-57088382
- Houses of the Oireachtas (Irish National Parliament),
  Joint Committee on Enterprise, Trade and Employment
  debate, 2021. 'Online content moderation: discussion',
  12/05. https://www.oireachtas.ie/en/debates/
  debate/joint_committee_on_enterprise_trade_and_
  employment/2021-05-12/2
- NewsTalk, quoting *The Hard Shoulder*, 2021. https://
  www.newstalk.com/news/i-can-see-it-in-my-dreams-
  facebook-moderator-calls-for-support-dealing-with-horrific-
  content-1193792

—Another relevant . . . will: The information on Meta's hiring and
salary policy comes from here:

- Newton, C., 2019. 'The Trauma Floor. The secret lives of
  Facebook moderators in America', *The Verge*, 25/02. https://
  www.theverge.com/2019/2/25/18229714/cognizant-
  facebook-content-moderator-interviews-trauma-working-
  conditions-arizona
- Newton, C., 2019. 'Bodies in Seats', *The Verge*, 19/06. https://
  www.theverge.com/2019/6/19/18681845/facebook-
  moderator-interviews-video-trauma-ptsd-cognizant-tampa

—Twitter . . . money: On subcontractors' operations outside Western
countries:

- Elliott, V. and Parmar, T., 2020. '"The despair and darkness of people will get to you"', Rest of World, 22/07. https://restofworld.org/2020/facebook-international-content-moderators

- Roberts, S.T., 2019. *Behind the Screen: content moderation in the shadows of social media*, Yale University Press.

—*One of them . . . exposure*: About Erin and Selena:

- Dwoskin, E., 2018. 'A content moderator says she got PTSD while reviewing images posted on Facebook', *Washington Post*, 24/09. https://www.washingtonpost.com/technology/2018/09/24/content-moderator-says-she-got-ptsd-while-reviewing-images-posted-facebook

- Wong, Q., 2019. 'Facebook faces complaints from more former content moderators in lawsuit', CNET, 01/03. https://www.cnet.com/tech/services-and-software/facebook-faces-complaints-from-more-content-moderators-in-lawsuit

The moderators' quotes are extracted from:

- Chen, A., 2014. 'The Laborers Who Keep Dick Pics and Beheadings Out of Your Facebook Feed', *Wired*, 23/10. https://www.wired.com/2014/10/content-moderation/

- Newton, 2019. 'The trauma floor'.

—*For centuries . . . time*: On the relationship between care work and the capitalist economy:

- Bhattacharya, T. (ed.), 2017. *Social Reproduction Theory: Remapping Class, Recentering Oppression*, Pluto Press.

—*Just to cite . . . laws:* On content moderation outside the West:

- Scott, M., 2021. 'Facebook did little to moderate posts in the world's most violent countries', *Politico*, 25/10. https://www.politico.com/news/2021/10/25/facebook-moderate-posts-violent-countries-517050

Chapter 2

—*In 2018 . . . claims*: Janey's story, together with those of other drivers, is reported here:

- Booth, R., 2021. 'Ex-Uber driver takes legal action over "racist" face-recognition software', *Guardian*, 05/10. https://www.theguardian.com/technology/2021/oct/05/ex-uber-driver-takes-legal-action-over-racist-face-recognition-software
- Melendez, S., 2018. Uber driver troubles raise concerns about transgender face recognition. *Fast Company*, 09/08. https://www.fastcompany.com/90216258/uber-face-recognition-tool-has-locked-out-some-transgender-drivers

About Uber and the sexual harassment of its female drivers and passengers:

- Statt, N., 2019. 'Uber's first ever safety report discloses 3,045 sexual assaults and nine murders in the US last year', *The Verge*, 05/12. https://www.theverge.com/2019/12/5/20997939/uber-safety-report-2018-sexual-assault-ride-hailing-platform-stats
- Uber, 2020. 'Uber launches Real-Time ID Check for drivers in the UK', 30/04. https://www.uber.com/en-GB/blog/real-time-id-check-uk-drivers

—*Recent research . . . the face*: Here are the studies and the reports I cite about facial-recognition software:

- Byrne-Haber, S., 2019. 'Disability and AI Bias', 11/07. https://sheribyrnehaber.medium.com/disability-and-ai-bias-cced271bd533
- Buolamwini, J. and Gebru, T., 2018. 'Gender Shades: Intersectional Accuracy Disparities in Commercial Gender Classification', *Proceedings of the 1st Conference on Fairness,*

Accountability and Transparency, PMLR, 81:77–91. https://
proceedings.mlr.press/v81/buolamwini18a.html

- Hamidi, F., Scheuerman, M.K. and Branham, S.M., 2018.
'Gender Recognition or Gender Reductionism?: The Social
Implications of Embedded Gender Recognition Systems',
*Proceedings of the 2018 Conference on Human Factors in Computing
Systems*, 8:1–13. doi: 10.1145/3173574.3173582
- Lohr, S., 2018. 'Facial recognition is accurate, if you're a white
guy'. In Martin, K. (ed.) *Ethics of Data and Analytics*, Auerbach,
143–47.

—*You have training . . . face*: On Joy Buolamwini's work:

- Germain, K. and Melguizo, M., 2017. 'A Search For
"Hidden Figures" Finds Joy', HuffPost, 28/02. https://
www.huffpost.com/entry/a-search-for-hidden-figures-finds-
joy_b_58b5f466e4b0e5fdf61977ef

—*In 2019 . . . race*: On Crystal Marie's vicissitudes and on The
Markup's study:

- Associated Press, 2021. 'How biased mortgage lending keeps
people of color locked out of dream homes', CBS News,
25/08. https://www.cbsnews.com/news/mortgage-lending-
algorithms-minorities-disparities
- Martinez, E. and Kirchner, L., 2021. 'How We Investigated
Racial Disparities in Federal Mortgage Data', The
Markup, 25/08. https://themarkup.org/show-your-
work/2021/08/25/how-we-investigated-racial-disparities-in-
federal-mortgage-data

—*In 2018 . . . years*: The Amazon algorithm saga is reported here:

- Dastin, J., 2018. 'Amazon scraps secret AI recruiting tool that
showed bias against women', Reuters, 11/10. https://www.

reuters.com/article/us-amazon-com-jobs-automation-insight-idUSKCN1MK08G

On Google algorithm's sexist and racist traits:

- Baker, P. and Potts, A., 2013. '"Why do white people have thin lips?"' Google and the perpetuation of stereotypes via auto-complete search forms', *Critical Discourse Studies*, 10(2) 187–204. doi: 10.1080/17405904.2012.744320
- Noble, S.U., 2018. *Algorithms of Oppression*, NY University Press.

—*Take . . . hope*: On Timnit Gebru's case:

- Tiku, N., 2020. 'Google hired Timnit Gebru to be an outspoken critic of unethical AI. Then she was fired for it', *Washington Post*, 23/12. https://www.washingtonpost.com/technology/2020/12/23/google-timnit-gebru-ai-ethics
- Simonite, T., 2021. 'What really happened when Google ousted Timnit Gebru', *Wired*, 08/06. https://www.wired.com/story/google-timnit-gebru-ai-what-really-happened
- Schwab, K., 2021. '"This is bigger than just Timnit": How Google tried to silence a critic and ignited a movement', *Fast Company*, 26/2. https://www.fastcompany.com/90608471/timnit-gebru-google-ai-ethics-equitable-tech-movement

—*In the United States . . . industries*: The stats capturing the inequalities rampant within the global tech industry are extrapolated from:

- BCS, The Chartered Institute for IT, 2020. *BCS Diversity Report 2020.*
- Daley, S., 2021. 'Women in Tech Statistics Show the Industry Has a Long Way to Go', Built In, 31/03. https://builtin.com/women-tech/women-in-tech-workplace-statistics
- Stack Overflow, 2020. 2020 Developer Survey. https://

insights.stackoverflow.com/survey/2020#developer-profile-disability-status-physical-differences

—*Let us start . . . corporation*: On Charlotte's and Chanin's cases and on the Amazon lawsuits:

- Del Rey, J., 2021. 'A Black Amazon manager is suing company executives in a discrimination and sexual harassment and assault case', Vox, 01/03. https://www.vox.com/recode/2021/3/1/22306508/amazon-race-discrimination-sexual-harassment-assault-lawsuit-charlotte-newman

- Greene, J., 2021. 'Five women sue Amazon for race and gender discrimination', *Independent*, 20/05. https://www.independent.co.uk/news/world/americas/amazon-women-gender-discrimination-b1850722.html

- Kelly-Rae, C., 2021. 'Amazon and Black liberation' [podcast], Living Corporate, 08/06. https://soundcloud.com/living-corporate/amazon-and-black-liberation-w-chanin-kelly-rae

—*Some of you . . . harassment*: Some sources on the strike and on Susan's story:

- Fowler, S., 2017. 'Reflecting On One Very, Very Strange Year At Uber', 19/2. https://www.susanjfowler.com/blog/2017/2/19/reflecting-on-one-very-strange-year-at-uber

- Fowler, S., 2020. 'I Spoke Out Against Sexual Harassment at Uber. The Aftermath Was More Terrifying Than Anything I Faced Before', *Time*, 17/02. https://time.com/5784464/susan-fowler-book-uber-sexual-harassment

- Google Walkout for Real Change, 2019. 'Onwards! Another #GoogleWalkout Goodbye', Medium, 16/07. https://googlewalkout.medium.com/onward-another-googlewalkout-goodbye-b733fa134a7d

- Weaver, M. et al., 2018. 'Google walkout: global protests after sexual misconduct allegations', *Guardian*, 01/11. https://www. theguardian.com/technology/2018/nov/01/google-walkout-global-protests-employees-sexual-harassment-scandals

—*For further confirmation . . . more at risk*: The report I mention is:

- Women Who Tech, 2020. *The State of Women in Tech and Startups. Top Findings For 2020*. https://womenwhotech.org/ data-and-resources/state-women-tech-and-startups

—*Academics . . . them*: The aphorism comes from Melvin Kranzberg:

- Kranzberg, M., 1986. 'Technology and History: "Kranzberg's Laws"', *Technology and Culture*. 27(3) 544–60. doi: 10.2307/3105385

—*Incidentally . . . men*: For a history of technology through a feminist lens:

- Wajcman, J., 2010. 'Feminist theories of technology', *Cambridge Journal of Economics*, 34(1) 143–52. doi: 10.1093/cje/ben057

Chapter 3

—*'My rapists . . . people'*: On Rose's story:

- House of Commons, Canada, 2021. Rose Kalemba's brief submitted to the Standing Committee on Access to Information, Privacy and Ethics, report: *Ensuring the Protection of Privacy and Reputation on Platforms Such as Pornhub*. https:// www.ourcommons.ca/Content/Committee/432/ETHI/ Brief/BR11156366/br-external/KalembaRose-e.pdf
- Kalemba, R., 2020. 'Re-Victimized: When Sexual Assault Gets Uploaded to Porn Platforms', *Model View Culture*, 14/04. https://modelviewculture.com/pieces/re-victimized-when-sexual-assault-gets-uploaded-to-porn-platforms

- Mohan, M., 2020. 'I was raped at 14, and the video ended up on a porn site', *BBC*, 10/2, https://www.bbc.co.uk/news/stories-51391981

Pornhub's former execs' quotes are taken from:

- House of Commons, Canada, 2021. *Ensuring the Protection of Privacy and Reputation on Platforms Such as Pornhub*, report of the Standing Committee on Access to Information, Privacy and Ethics. https://www.ourcommons.ca/Content/Committee/432/ETHI/Reports/RP11148202/ethirp03/ethirp03-e.pdf

—*In 2019 . . . years*: Some useful sources on MindGeek, from which I have derived the data I cite, are:

- Bradley-Smith, A., 2021. '34 Women Claim Pornhub Profited Off Videos of Them It Posted Without Their Consent', Top Class Actions, 18/6. https://topclassactions.com/lawsuit-settlements/sexual-assault-abuse/34-women-claim-pornhub-profited-off-videos-of-them-it-posted-without-their-consent

- Castaldo, J., 2021. 'Lifting the veil of secrecy on MindGeek's online pornography empire', *Globe and Mail*, 04/02. https://www.theglobeandmail.com/business/article-mindgeeks-business-practices-under-srutiny-as-political-pressure

- The Internet Watch Foundation, 2018. Once Upon A Year – Annual Report 2018. https://www.iwf.org.uk/media/tthh3woi/once-upon-a-year-iwf-annual-report-2018.pdf

- U.S. District Court for the Central District of California, 2021. *Serena Fleites et al v. MindGeek S.A.R.L. et al*. Filed lawsuit. https://dockets.justia.com/docket/california/cacdce/2:2021cv04920/823614

—The most notorious . . . advertisements: About Hunter Moore and other non-consensual pornography websites:

- Hearn, J. and Hall, M., 2019. 'This is my cheating ex': Gender and sexuality in revenge porn. *Sexualities*, 22(5–6) 860–82. doi: 10.1177/1363460718779965
- Lee, D., 2012, 'Is Anyone's Up's Hunter Moore: "The Net's Most Hated Man"', BBC, 20/4. https://www.bbc.co.uk/news/technology-17784232
- Morris, A., 2012. 'Hunter Moore: The Most Hated Man on the Internet', *Rolling Stone*, 11/10. https://www.rollingstone.com/culture/culture-news/hunter-moore-the-most-hated-man-on-the-internet-184668

- Hunter Moore's own quote is extracted from:

- Dodero, C., 2012. 'Hunter Moore makes a living screwing you', *The Village Voice*, 4/4/. https://www.villagevoice.com/2012/04/04/hunter-moore-makes-a-living-screwing-you

—Even . . . page 212 (footnote): On the relationship between porn tubes and sex work:

- Boone, L., 2022. '"Because of Sex"', *North Carolina Law Review*, 100(3), 883.
- Rothman, E.F., 2021. *Pornography and Public Health*. Oxford University Press.

—First . . . films: On the popularity of online rape scenes:

- Makin, D.A. and Morczek, A.L., 2015. 'The Dark Side of Internet Searches: A Macro Level Assessment of Rape Culture', *International Journal of Cyber Criminology*, 9(1) 1–23. doi: 10.5281/zenodo.22057

—*How do . . . model*: On MindGeek's reactions to recent scandals:

• Maiberg. E., 2021. 'MindGeek Shuts Down Porn Tube Site XTube', Vice, 07/07. https://www.vice.com/en/article/dyv4km/mindgeek-shuts-down-porn-tube-site-xtube

• Paul, K., 2020. 'Pornhub removes millions of videos after investigation finds child abuse content', *Guardian*, 14/12. https://www.theguardian.com/technology/2020/dec/14/pornhub-purge-removes-unverified-videos-investigation-child-abuse?fbclid=IwAR15n8ntnIA6FFtktoeIp2PYzIrgWTAbR7z VYdHI-yH_g1Tuvmc8-oATknw

—*This woman . . . them*: About Mirindi's story:

• Taylor, D., 2008. 'Aged one to 90: the victims of hidden war against women', *Guardian*, 05/12. https://www.theguardian.com/world/2008/dec/05/congo-rape-testimonies-walungu

—*Mirindi . . . abuse*: On war rapes and conflicts in the DRC and on their link with the mineral supply chain, I recommend:

• Baaz, M.E. and Stern, M., 2013. *Sexual Violence as a Weapon of War?: Perceptions, Prescriptions, Problems in the Congo and Beyond*, Bloomsbury.

• Kirby, P., 2013. How is rape a weapon of war? Feminist International Relations, modes of critical explanation and the study of wartime sexual violence. *European Journal of International Relations*, 19(4) 797–821. doi: 10.1177/1354066111427614

—*In 2017 . . . all'*: The testimonies of the survivors interviewed by MSF can be found here:

• Voices from the field, 2018. '"When I tell this story, I see a film playing before my eyes"', Médecins Sans Frontières, 01/11.

https://www.msf.org/drc-when-i-tell-story-i-see-film-playing-my-eyes

—*Among . . . survivors*: On Dr Denis Mukwege and Christine Schuler Deschryver:

* Mukwege, D., 2022. *The Power of Women*, Macmillan.

—*I wish . . . all'*:

* Taylor, D., 2011. 'Congo rape victims face slavery in gold and mineral mines', *Guardian*, 02/09. https://www.theguardian.com/world/2011/sep/02/congo-women-face-slavery-mines#:~:text=Rape%20victims%20in%20eastern%20Democratic,a%20Guardian%20investigation%20has%20found.

—*And to be fair . . . country*: On the contradictory effects of existing regulations:

* Stoop, N., Verpoorten, M. and van der Windt, P., 2018. 'More legislation, more violence? The impact of Dodd-Frank in the DRC', PloS ONE, 13(8) e0201783. doi: 10.1371/journal.pone.0201783
* International Peace Information Service and Danish Institute for International Studies, 2019. *Mapping artisanal mining areas and mineral supply chains in eastern DR Congo: Impact of armed interference & responsible sourcing*, D/2019/4320/07. https://ipisresearch.be/wp-content/uploads/2019/04/1904-IOM-mapping-eastern-DRC_versie03.pdf

—*'I'm not healthy . . . whole*: The accounts from women miners, together with the other details about mining in the DRC, can be found here:

* Amnesty International, 2016. 'Child labour behind smart phone and electric car batteries', 19/01. https://www.

amnesty.org/en/latest/news/2016/01/Child-labour-behind-smart-phone-and-electric-car-batteries

- Niarchos, N., 2021. 'The Dark Side of Congo's Cobalt Rush', *New Yorker*, 24/05. https://www.newyorker.com/magazine/2021/05/31/the-dark-side-of-congos-cobalt-rush
- Taylor, 'Congo rape victims'.
- Wolfe, L., 2015. 'Raped for slave wages: Women in Congo trapped in under-reported violence amid "conflict minerals"'. Women's Media Center, 13/02. https://womensmediacenter.com/women-under-siege/congo-women-raped-underreported-violence-conflict-minerals

—*For centuries . . . masters*: On the role played by the exploitation of women's bodies within the history of capitalism:

- Federici, S., 2004. *Caliban and the Witch*, Autonomedia.
- Penny, L., 2011. *Meat Market*, Calton.

Chapter 4

—*Tiziana . . . scarf*: Sources for Tiziana's story:

- D'Angelo, S., 2019. 'Il caso Tiziana Cantone, i social network e la web reputation', *Il Diritto*, 01/04. https://www.diritto.it/il-caso-tiziana-cantone-i-social-network-e-la-web-reputation
- *Fatto Quotidiano*, 2016. 'Tiziana Cantone: La denuncia ai PM', 16/09. https://www.ilfattoquotidiano.it/2016/09/16/tiziana-cantone-la-denuncia-ai-pm-quei-video-mi-stanno-rovinando-la-vita/3037244
- Warren, R., 2018. 'A Mother Wants the Internet to Forget Italy's Most Viral Sex Tape', *The Atlantic*, 16/5. https://www.theatlantic.com/technology/archive/2018/05/tiziana-cantone-suicide-right-to-be-forgotten/559289

Maria Teresa's considerations are extracted from:

- Farace, R. and Ribustini, L., 2019. *Uccisa dal web: Tiziana Cantone*, Jouvence.

—*Even Google . . . regulations*: On the relationship between Google and the spreading of non-consensual pornography:

- Fonrouge, G., 2018. 'Google has history of failing to remove revenge porn: lawyers', *New York Post*, 21/06. https://nypost.com/2018/06/21/google-has-history-of-failing-to-remove-revenge-porn-lawyers
- Goldberg, C., 2019. 'How Google has destroyed the lives of revenge porn victims', *New York Post*, 17/08. https://nypost.com/2019/08/17/how-google-has-destroyed-the-lives-of-revenge-porn-victims/amp/?__twitter_impression=true

—*Contrary . . . machine*: This very mechanism is well-described in:

- Seymour, R., 2019. *The Twittering Machine*, Indigo Press.

—*We are aware . . . wrong*: About Frances Haugen's saga:

- Haugen, F., 2021. *Whistleblower Aid: Statement of Frances Haugen*, 4/10. https://www.commerce.senate.gov/services/files/FC8A558E-824E-4914-BEDB-3A7B1190BD49
- Horwitz, J., 2021. 'The Facebook Whistleblower, Frances Haugen, Says She Wants to Fix the Company, Not Harm It', *Wall Street Journal*, 03/10. https://www.wsj.com/articles/facebook-whistleblower-frances-haugen-says-she-wants-to-fix-the-company-not-harm-it-11633304122
- Perrigo, B., 2021. 'How Facebook Forced a Reckoning by Shutting Down the Team That Put People Ahead of Profits', *Time*, 07/10. https://time.com/6104899/facebook-reckoning-frances-haugen

—*In the light . . . persecution*: On Facebook's reaction to Tiziana's death:

- Beneduce, T., 2016. 'Tiziana, suicida per i filmati hard. Facebook presenta ricorso sui video', *Corriere del Mezzogiorno*, 05/10. https://corrieredelmezzogiorno.corriere.it/napoli/cronaca/16_ottobre_05/tiziana-suicida-filmati-hard-facebook-presenta-ricorso-video-5d71c182-8ac0-11e6-bc2b-cc56a2496646.shtml

—*but I will . . . goals*: On Google's search algorithm manipulation:

- Grind, K., et al., 2019. 'How Google Interferes With Its Search Algorithms and Changes Your Results', *Wall Street Journal*, 15/11. https://www.wsj.com/articles/how-google-interferes-with-its-search-algorithms-and-changes-your-results-11573823753

—*Just consider . . . media*: The sources of the data I cite are:

- Balocco, V., 2021. 'Informazione online, oltre 4 milioni di italiani si informano solo sui social', *CorCom*, 28/12. https://www.corrierecomunicazioni.it/media/informazione-online-oltre-4-milioni-di-italiani-si-informano-solo-sui-social-network

- Ofcom, 2019. 'Half of people now get their news from social media', 24/07. https://www.ofcom.org.uk/about-ofcom/latest/features-and-news/half-of-people-get-news-from-social-media

—*Gradually . . . attacks*: Among such studies, I recommend:

- Henry, N., Powell, A. and Flynn, A., 2017. *Not Just 'Revenge Pornography': Australians' Experiences of Image-Based Abuse: A Summary Report*, RMIT University, Melbourne.

- Kamal, M. and Newman, W.J., 2016. 'Revenge Pornography:

Mental Health Implications and Related Legislation', *Journal of the American Academy of Psychiatry and the Law*, 44(3), 359–67.

- World Wide Web Foundation, 2020. 'The online crisis facing women and girls threatens global progress on gender equality', 12/03. https://webfoundation.org/2020/03/the-online-crisis-facing-women-and-girls-threatens-global-progress-on-gender-equality

Chapter 5

—*One night . . . toilet*: On gig workers' strike against Urban Company:

- Ara, I., 2021. 'Urban Company Sues Workers for Protesting Against "Unfair Labour Practices". Protest Called Off', *The Wire*, 23/12. https://thewire.in/rights/urban-company-sues-workers-for-protesting-against-unfair-labour-practices-protest-called-off
- Mathew, S., 2022. 'Brewing Up A Revolution On WhatsApp', Feminism in India, 28/02. https://feminisminindia.com/2022/02/28/urban-company-beauty-partners-women-whatsapp-revolution
- Reuters, 2021. 'In a first, Urban Company sues protesting women workers', *Business Today.In*, 23/12. https://www.businesstoday.in/latest/corporate/story/in-a-first-urban-company-sues-protesting-women-workers-316660-2021-12-23

—*In 2020 . . . come*: The cited data is extrapolated from:

- Huws et al., 2017. *Work in the European Gig Economy*, FEPS in cooperation with UNI Europa and the University of Hertfordshire. https://uhra.herts.ac.uk/bitstream/

handle/2299/19922/Huws_U._Spencer_N.H._Syrdal_D.S._ Holt_K._2017_.pdf

• Mastercard and Kaiser Associates, 2019. *The Global Gig Economy*. https://newsroom.mastercard.com/wp-content/ uploads/2019/05/Gig-Economy-White-Paper-May-2019.pdf

• Mohanty, P., 2021. 'Gig economy: Good for companies, bad for workers', *Fortune India*, 31/12. https://www.fortuneindia. com/opinion/gig-economy-good-for-companies-bad-for- workers/106569

—*Where there . . . possible*: Some sources on women drivers and riders:

• Cook, C. et al., 2018. *The Gender Earnings Gap in the Gig Economy: Evidence from over a Million Rideshare Drivers*, working paper 3637, Graduate School of Stanford, Business, 07/06. https://www.gsb.stanford.edu/faculty-research/working- papers/gender-earnings-gap-gig-economy-evidence-over- million-rideshare

• Gurmat, S., 2021. 'No bathrooms, no safety, no formalisation: For India's women gig-workers, companies' promises ring hollow', *The Leaflet*, 18/10. https://theleaflet.in/no- bathrooms-no-safety-no-formalisation-for-indias-women-gig- workers-companies-promises-ring-hollow/?fbclid=IwAR2xzZ LaKfrstQLaf0iWrw8Rx-zpocP9WNM8uNvBLUjA74m9nKt_ fHkk7i0

—*A paradigmatic . . . associations*: Sources on gig care workers:

• Rathi, A. and Tandon, A., 2021. *Platforms, Power, and Politics: Perspectives from Domestic and Care Work in India*, Centre for Internet & Society, 27/06. https://cis-india.org/raw/

platforms-power-and-politics-perspectives-from-domestic-and-care-work-in-india

- Ticona, J. et al., 2018. *Beyond disruption. How tech shapes labor across domestic work & ridehailing*, Data & Society, 27/06. https://datasociety.net/library/beyond-disruption

- Young, N., 2021. 'The global gig workers', Rest of World, 21/9. https://restofworld.org/2021/global-gig-workers-on-demand-cleaner-south-africa

—*Not even . . . conditions*: On the online therapy industry:

- Karlis, N., 2019. 'The gig economy comes for therapists', *Salon*, 15/03. https://www.salon.com/2019/03/15/the-gig-economy-comes-for-therapists

—*Nellie . . . activities*: Influencers' and digital creatives' testimonies are extracted from here:

- Kleeman, J., 2019. '"We can't reach the women who need us": the LGBT YouTubers suing the tech giant for discrimination', *Guardian*, 14/08. https://www.theguardian.com/technology/2019/aug/14/youtube-bria-kam-chrissy-chambers-lesbian-vloggers-lgbtq-discrimination

- Tait, A., 2020. '"Influencers are being taken advantage of": the social media stars turning to unions', *Guardian*, 10/10. https://www.theguardian.com/media/2020/oct/10/influencers-are-being-taken-advantage-of-the-social-media-stars-turning-to-unions

- The information about Speakr (including some influencers' accusations that the platform delayed their payment) is exactrated from:

- Lorenz, T., 2018. 'When a Sponsored Facebook Post Doesn't Pay Off', *The Atlantic*, 26/12. https://www.

theatlantic.com/technology/archive/2018/12/massive-influencer-management-platform-has-been-stiffing-people-payments/578767

—*For a start . . . women*: The data on the influencer economy comes from:

- Influencer Marketing Hub, *The State of Influencer Marketing 2022: Benchmark Report*. https://influencermarketinghub.com/influencer-marketing-benchmark-report

- Statista Research Department, 2019. 'Distribution of influencers creating sponsored posts on Instagram worldwide in 2019, by gender', Statista. https://www.statista.com/statistics/893749/share-influencers-creating-sponsored-posts-by-gender

—*For these . . . guidelines*: About digital creatives' organising:

- Ashley, B., 2020. 'Why Instagram influencers are unionising', *Vogue Business*, 13/7. https://www.voguebusiness.com/companies/why-instagram-influencers-are-unionising

—*Several . . . ruthlessly*: On the concept of prosumption:

- Ritzer G. and Jurgenson N., 2010. 'Production, Consumption, Prosumption: The nature of capitalism in the age of the digital "prosumer"', *Journal of Consumer Culture*, 10(1) 13–36. doi: 10.1177/1469540509354673

Here are the details of Shoshana Zuboff's volume:

- Zuboff, S., 2019. *The Age of Surveillance Capitalism*, Profile Books.

—*What's . . . rights*: On the 'what's work?' debate, and on its developments in the digital era:

- Federici, S., 2020. *Revolution at Point Zero: Housework, Reproduction, and Feminist Struggle*, PM Press

• Jarrett, K., 2015. *Feminism, Labour and Digital Media: The Digital Housewife*, Routledge.

• Terranova, T., 2000. 'Free Labor: Producing Culture for the Digital Economy', *Social Text*, 18(2) 33–58. doi: 10.1215/01642472-18-2_63-33

Chapter 6

—In 2020 . . . spring 2020: Information on *FT* piece:

• *Financial Times*, 2020. 'Prospering in the pandemic: the top 100 companies', 19/06. https://www.ft.com/content/844ed28c-8074-4856-bde0-20f3bf4cd8f0

—Digital violence . . . apps: On online abuse in the Covid era:

• Elmer G. et al., 2021. 'Zoombombing During a Global Pandemic', *Social Media + Society*. doi: 10.1177/20563051211035356

• Petter, O., 2021. 'One in four women say cyberflashing has increased during pandemic', *Independent*, 02/11. https://www.independent.co.uk/life-style/women/cyberflashing-bumble-illegal-unsolicited-b1949158.html

• Statista Research Department, 2022. *Annual direct revenue of Tinder from 2015 to 2020*, Statista. https://www.statista.com/statistics/1101990/tinder-global-direct-revenue

• UN Women, 2020. *Online and ICT-facilitated violence against women and girls during Covid-19*. https://www.unwomen.org/en/digital-library/publications/2020/04/brief-online-and-ict-facilitated-violence-against-women-and-girls-during-covid-19

—Take . . . Capitol: On the impact of Instagram use on teenage girls:

• Kleemans, M. et al., 2018. 'Picture Perfect: The Direct

Effect of Manipulated Instagram Photos on Body Image
in Adolescent Girls', *Media Psychology*, 21(1) 93–110.
doi: 10.1080/15213269.2016.1257392

- Milmo, D. and Paul, K., 2021. 'Facebook harms children
and is damaging democracy, claims whistleblower', *Guardian*,
06/10. https://www.theguardian.com/technology/2021/
oct/05/facebook-harms-children-damaging-democracy-
claims-whistleblower

—*Judging from . . . distress*: The data about women smart workers
can be found here:

- Andrew, A., et al, 2020. 'How are mothers and fathers
balancing work and family under lockdown?', Institute for
Fiscal Studies, 27/05. https://ifs.org.uk/publications/14860
- McKinsey & Co., 2021. 'Women in the Workplace 2021',
27/09. https://www.mckinsey.com/featured-insights/
diversity-and-inclusion/women-in-the-workplace
- Office for National Statistics, 2020. 'Parenting
in lockdown', 22/07. https://www.ons.
gov.uk/peoplepopulationandcommunity/
healthandsocialcare/conditionsanddiseases/articles/
parentinginlockdowncoronavirusandtheeffectson
worklifebalance/2020-07-22

—*Just like . . . Watch*: The source used for this section:

- Human Rights Watch, 2021. '"I Had Nowhere to Go":
Violence Against Women and Girls During the Covid-19
Pandemic in Kenya', 21/09. https://www.hrw.org/
report/2021/09/21/i-had-nowhere-go/violence-against-
women-and-girls-during-covid-19-pandemic-kenya

—*This should . . . because of it*: The figures and testimonies of the Kenyan digital gap come from:

- GSMA, 2021. *Connected Women*: *The Mobile Gender Gap Report 2021.* https://www.gsma.com/r/wp-content/uploads/2021/07/The-Mobile-Gender-Gap-Report-2021.pdf
- Human Rights Watch, 2020. *Impact of Covid-19 on Children's Education in Africa*, 26/08. https://www.hrw.org/news/2020/08/26/impact-covid-19-childrens-education-africa#_edn39

—*According . . . geography*: The studies I cite are:

- A4AI, 2021. *The Costs Of Exclusion. Economic Consequences of the Digital Gender Gap.* https://a4ai.org/research/costs-of-exclusion-report
- Plan International, 2020. 'Time for Change. COVID-19, Connectivity and Equality', 06/05. https://plan-international.org/blog/2020/05/06/time-for-change-covid-19-connectivity-and-equality

—*In Pakistan . . . together*: Here are the various reports I mention:

- Children's Commissioner, 2020. 'Children without internet access during lockdown', 18/08. https://www.childrenscommissioner.gov.uk/2020/08/18/children-without-internet-access-during-lockdown
- GSMA, 2020. *The Digital Exclusion of Women with Disabilities.* https://www.gsma.com/mobilefordevelopment/wp-content/uploads/2020/07/GSMA_Digital-Exclusion-of-Women-with-Disabilities_44pp_ACCESSIBLE.pdf
- Media Matters for Democracy, 2021. *Women Disconnected: Feminist Case Studies on the Gender Digital Divide Amidst COVID-19.* http://www.digitalrightsmonitor.pk/wp-content/

uploads/2021/01/Women-Disconnected-Gender-Digital-
Divide-in-Pakistan.pdf
- Office of National Statistics, 2019. *Exploring the
UK's digital divide*, 04/03. https://www.ons.gov.uk/
peoplepopulationandcommunity/householdcharacteristics/
homeinternetandsocialmediausage/articles/
exploringtheuksdigitaldivide/2019-03-04
- Young Lives and University of Oxford, 2021. *Young Lives at
Work*. https://www.younglives.org.uk/research-project/young-
lives-work

—*In autumn . . . Musk*: Sources for the Salinas picture, the digital
gender gap in the USA, as well as *Forbes*'s study:

- Budryk, Z., 2020. 'Viral photo of girls using Taco Bell WiFi
to do homework highlights "digital divide"', *The Hill*, 02/09.
https://thehill.com/blogs/blog-briefing-room/news/514905-
viral-photo-of-girls-using-taco-bell-wifi-to-do-homework
- Cai, K., 2021, 'Golden State Billionaires', *Forbes*, 06/04.
- Common Sense Media, 2020. *Closing the K-12 Digital Divide in
the Age of Distance Learning*. https://www.commonsensemedia.
org/sites/default/files/featured-content/files/common_
sense_media_report_final_7_1_3pm_web.pdf
- LeanIn.org and Survey Monkey, 2020. *Impact of COVID-19
on Women*. https://docs.google.com/document/d/19UkIM_
LtTUj02El9Hw7U03-ybv0sCGUNTYGdnrHz7FU/edit#

Chapter 7

—*In summer . . . protocol*: On Gamergate and its political
implications:

- Lees, M., 2016. 'What Gamergate should have taught

us about the "alt-right"', *Guardian*, 01/12. https://www.
theguardian.com/technology/2016/dec/01/gamergate-alt-
right-hate-trump

- Romano, A. 2021. 'What we still haven't learned from
  Gamergate', Vox, 07/01. https://www.vox.com/
  culture/2020/1/20/20808875/gamergate-lessons-cultural-
  impact-changes-harassment-laws

Milo Yannopoulos's quote is extracted from here:

- Jilani, Z., 2014. 'Gamergate's fickle hero: The dark
  opportunism of Breitbart's Milo Yannopoulos', 28/10.
  https://www.salon.com/2014/10/28/gamergates_
  fickle_hero_the_dark_opportunism_of_breitbarts_milo_
  yiannopoulos

Mike Cernovich's piece on choking can be found here:

- Cernovich, M., 2011. 'How to choke a woman', *Danger & Play:
  An Online Magazine for Alpha Males*, 26/12. https://web.archive.
  org/web/20130604101419/https://www.dangerandplay.
  com/2011/12/26/how-to-choke-a-woman

His tweet on date rape, posted on the 12th of August 2012, is
reported here:

- Nashrulla, T., 2017. 'Donald Trump Jr Showered Praise
  on this Rape Apologist', *BuzzFeed*, 4/4. https://www.
  buzzfeednews.com/article/tasneemnashrulla/donald-trump-
  jr-said-this-rape-apologist-deserves-a-pultizer

On the 'manosphere':

- Bates, L., 2020. *Men Who Hate Women*, Simon & Schuster.

About Ilhan Omar incident:

- Rupar, A., 2019. 'Trump retweets lie that Ilhan Omar
  "partied" on 9/11 anniversary', Vox, 18/09. https://www.

vox.com/2019/9/18/20872316/trump-ilhan-omar-9-11-
partied-retweet-terrence-williams

—*When he . . . excitement*: On the Italian, Brazilian, Indian, US and
Russian examples I mention:

* Ayyub, R., 2018. 'I Was The Victim Of A Deepfake
  Porn Plot Intended To Silence Me', HuffPost, 21/11.
  https://www.huffingtonpost.co.uk/entry/deepfake-porn_
  uk_5bf2c126e4b0f32bd58ba316
* *La Stampa*, 2014. '"Cosa faresti in auto con Boldrini?"', 01/02.
  https://www.lastampa.it/politica/2014/02/01/news/cosa-
  faresti-in-auto-con-la-boldrini-1.35919582
* Lomko, I. et al., 2009. 'The Kremlin's virtual squad',
  openDemocracy, 19/03. https://www.opendemocracy.net/
  en/the-kremlins-virtual-squad
* *Redazione* (editorial board), 2018. 'Salvini, minorenni
  "in pasto" sui social', *Affari Italiani* 21/11. https://www.
  affaritaliani.it/milano/salvini-minorenni-in-pasto-sui-social-la-
  protesta-nelle-scuole-milanesi-573282.html
* *Redazione* (editorial board), 2019. 'Dalla Boldrini a Carola
  Rackete: donne nel mirino della violenza social', *Pickline*,
  01/07. https://pickline.it/2019/06/30/dalla-boldrini-a-
  carola-donne-nel-mirino-della-violenza-social
* Suárez, E., 2021. 'You can't blame platforms alone, but in
  a country with the right conditions they can undermine
  democracy and public debate', Reuters Institute, University
  of Oxford, 04/06. https://reutersinstitute.politics.ox.ac.
  uk/news/you-cant-blame-platforms-alone-country-right-
  conditions-they-can-undermine-democracy-and

The Deeptrace report on deepfakes I cite:

- Ajder, H. et al., 2019. *The State of Deepfake: Landscape, Threats, and Impact.* https://regmedia.co.uk/2019/10/08/deepfake_report.pdf

Steve Bannon's quote comes from here:

- Snider, M., 2017. 'Steve Bannon learned to harness trolls from "World of Warcraft"', *USA Today*, 18/07. https://eu.usatoday.com/story/tech/talkingtech/2017/07/18/steve-bannon-learned-harness-troll-army-world-warcraft/489713001

—*To shed . . . voices*: Links to the pictures I mention:

- Carlson, N., 2011. 'Obama's dinner with America's tech leaders', Insider, 18/02. https://www.businessinsider.com/people-at-obamas-tech-dinner-2011-2?r=US&IR=T#economists-hang-on-john-chamberss-every-word-3
- Dayen, D., 2016. 'The Android Administration: Google's Remarkably Close Relationship With the Obama White House, in Two Charts', The Intercept, 22/04. https://theintercept.com/2016/04/22/googles-remarkably-close-relationship-with-the-obama-white-house-in-two-charts
- D'Onfro, J., 2018. 'The Saudi Crown Prince hung out this week with Google execs Sergey Brin and Sundar Pichai', CNBC, 07/04. https://www.cnbc.com/2018/04/07/heres-a-look-at-who.html
- ParlamentoNews, 2016. 'Renzi incontra CEO Amazon Jeff Bezos' [video], YouTube, 25/07. https://www.youtube.com/watch?v=iUQuOOUKPM4
- *Redazione* (editorial board), 2016. 'Renzi gives Zuckerberg Cicero's On Friendship', ANSA, 29/08. https://www.ansa.it/

english/news/2016/08/29/renzi-gives-zuckerberg-ciceros-on-friendship_9018e5a6-c966-45b2-a267-281e9d46ae60.html

- Whichit, 2015. 'British Technology Entrepreneurs Reception at 10 Downing Street', blogpost, *Whichit.co*, 19/10. https://whichit.co/blog/2015/10/19/british-technology-entrepreneurs-reception-at-10-downing-street

—*I assume . . . about*: On Cambridge Analytica:

- Wylie, C., 2020. *Mind f*ck: Inside Cambridge Analytica's Plot to Break the World*, Profile Books.

—*Nonetheless . . . fields*: On gender disparities within decision-making bodies and their impact over sensitive policies:

- BBC, 2017. 'All-male White House health bill photo sparks anger', BBC News, 24/03. https://www.bbc.co.uk/news/world-us-canada-39375228
- Durkin, E. and Benwell, M., 2019. 'These 25 Republicans – all white men – just voted to ban abortion in Alabama', *Guardian*, 15/05. https://www.theguardian.com/us-news/2019/may/14/alabama-abortion-ban-white-men-republicans
- Inter-Parliamentary Union, 2022. *Women In Parliament 2021*. https://www.ipu.org/resources/publications/reports/2022-03/women-in-parliament-in-2021

Justice for Men and Boys' policy proposals can be read here:

- Buchanan, M., 2015. *Justice for Men and Boys (and the Women Who Love Them), 2015 General Election Manifesto*, LPS Publishing.

—*Let us . . . use*: On the Absher app case:

- Human Rights Watch, 2019. 'Saudi Arabia's Absher App', 06/05. https://www.hrw.org/news/2019/05/06/saudiarabias-absher-app-controlling-womens-travel-while-offering-government

—*Rivers of ink . . . to make them*: Among these various studies, I suggest in particular:

- Chomsky, N., 1999. *Profit Over People*, Seven Stories Press.
- Fraser, N., 2013. *Fortunes of Feminism: From State-Managed Capitalism to Neoliberal Crisis*, Verso.

Chapter 8

—*If you had happened . . . Wikipedia*: On sexism within Wikipedia and the editathons:

- Newnham College, 2017. 'Newnham holds Wikipedia edit-a-thon to make the internet less sexist on International Women's Day', 09/03. https://newn.cam.ac.uk/newnham-news/newnham-hosts-wikipedia-edit-thon-make-internet-less-sexist-international-womens-day
- Tripodi, F., 2021. 'Ms. Categorized: Gender, notability, and inequality on Wikipedia', *New Media & Society*, 27/06, 1–21. doi: 10.1177/14614448211023772

—*Or to fear . . . house*: Audre Lorde's quote comes from:

- Lorde, A., 1984. *Sister Outsider*, Crossing Press.

—*It is not . . . divisive*: See:

- Firestone, S., 1970. *The Dialectic of Sex*, William Morrow and Company.
- Haraway, D., 1985. 'A Manifesto for Cyborgs: Science, Technology and Socialist Feminism in the 1980s', *Socialist Review* (80), 65–108.

—*The first . . . future*: Some sources behind my three examples are:

- Brice, M., 2012. 'Postpartum: Mainichi – How Personal

Experience Became a Game', 11/11. http://www.mattiebrice.
com/postpartum-mainichi-how-personal-experience-became-
a-game

- Haimson, O.L. et al., 2021. 'Tumblr was a trans technology:
the meaning, importance, history, and future of trans
technologies', *Feminist Media Studies*, 21(3), 345–361.
doi: 10.1080/14680777.2019.1678505
- Kennedy, H.W., 2002. 'Lara Croft: Feminist Icon or
Cyberbimbo?: On the Limits of Textual Analysis', *Game
Studies*, 2(2). http://gamestudies.org/0202/kennedy
- Khaw, C., 2014. 'The internet fixes Barbie's "I Can Be a
Computer Engineer" picture book', *The Verge*, 19/11. https://
www.theverge.com/2014/11/19/7245461/feminist-barbie-
hacker-engineer-fix

—*Suppose . . . more*: On World Pulse and All Out:

- Afzal, S., 2013. 'Digital Connections Empower Women to
Change Their Futures', Mashable, 23/09. https://mashable.
com/archive/world-pulse-activist-congo#J..5MuBW7Pky
- All Out, 2022. 'Russia: LGBT+ Activist Under House Arrest'.
https://action.allout.org/en/a/yulja
- Epatko, L., 2013. 'World Pulse's "web" of women keeps
growing', *PBS NewsHour*, 30/09. https://www.pbs.org/
newshour/world/world-pulse

—*Before . . . problems*: On disability justice movements and their
contributions to design, and generally on participatory design for
social justice:

- Costanza-Chock, S., 2018. 'Design Justice: towards an
intersectional feminist framework for design theory and
practice', in Storni, C., Leahy, K., McMahon, M., Lloyd,

P. and Bohemia, E. (eds), *Design as a catalyst for change – DRS International Conference 2018*, 25–28 June. doi: 10.21606/drs.2018.679

- Costanza-Chock, S., 2020. 'Design Practices: "Nothing about Us without Us"', *Design Justice: Community-Led Practices to Build the Worlds We Need*, MIT Press. doi: 10.7551/mitpress/12255.003.0006

- Girma, H., 2017. 'People with Disabilities Drive Innovation', *Financial Times*, 13/09. https://www.ft.com/content/d8997604-97ab-11e7-8c5c-c8d8fa6961bb

—*Except . . . permission*: On pinkwashing and period apps:

- Healy, R.L., 2021. 'Zuckerberg, get out of my uterus! An examination of fertility apps, data-sharing and remaking the female body as a digitalized reproductive subject', *Journal of Gender Studies*, 30(4), 406–416. doi: 10.1080/09589236.2020.1845628

—*The first . . . future:* On feminist tech design and feminist hacker cultures:

- Feminist Internet and Josie Young, 2021. *Feminist Design Tool*, UGC Future Learn. https://ugc.futurelearn.com/uploads/files/16/b0/16b088ad-6145-45eb-b5d8-3753a41b4b88/2-10_FeministDesignTool_2.0.pdf

- Schofield, D., 2019. 'Understanding bias in AI with the help of a feminist chatbot', *Dazed*, 23/05. https://www.dazeddigital.com/science-tech/article/44489/1/understanding-ai-bias-feminist-internet-chatbot-alexa-f-xa

- Toupin, S., 2014. Feminist Hackerspaces: The Synthesis of Feminist and Hacker Cultures. *Journal of Peer Production*, 5(2014) 1–11.

Chapter 9

—*Evgeny . . . struggles*: On solutionism:

- Morozov, E., 2019. *To Save Everything, Click Here*, Allen Lane.

—*Prevent . . . TikTok*: To know more on my proposals on how to address digital gender-based violence:

- Citron, D.K., 2014. *Hate Crimes in Cyberspace*, Harvard University Press.
- GenPol: Gender & Policy Insights, 2019. *When Technology Meets Misogyny. Multilevel, Intersectional Solutions to Digital Gender-based Violence.*
- Judson, E., 2022. *The Online Safety Bill: Demos Position Paper*, 01/04. https://demos.co.uk/project/the-online-safety-bill-demos-position-paper
- McGlynn, C. et al., 2017. 'Beyond "revenge porn": The Continuum of Image-Based Sexual Abuse', *Feminist Legal Studies*, 25(1) 25–46. doi: 10.1007/s10691-017-9343-2

—*Mainstream . . . matter*: On the DSA and other regulations under discussion:

- Amnesty International, 2021. 'Position on the Proposals for a DSA and a DMA', 30/03. https://www.amnesty.eu/wp-content/uploads/2021/04/Amnesty-International-Position-Paper-Digital-Services-Act-Package_March2021_Updated.pdf
- European Commission, 2021. 'Questions & answers. Reinforcing democracy and integrity of elections', 25/11.
- Fazlioglu, M., 2021. 'Next-gen privacy', IAPP, 17/02. https://iapp.org/news/a/nextgen-privacy-the-eus-eprivacy-regulation
- Prtorić, J., 2022. 'EU's amended DSA fails to better regulate "revenge porn"', OpenDemocracy, 13/05. https://www.

opendemocracy.net/en/5050/revenge-porn-european-union-digital-services-act

—*This is why . . . gender*: On tax reforms and addressing digital monopolies:

- Center for Humane Technology, 2022. Policy Reforms Toolkit. https://www.humanetech.com/policy-reforms
- Fuchs, C., 2019. *The Online Advertising Tax as the Foundation of a Public Service Internet*, CAMRI, 02/01. https://camri.ac.uk/blog/articles/the-online-advertising-tax-as-the-foundation-of-a-public-service-internet
- Silkin, L., 2019. 'Robot Tax: The Pros and Cons of Taxing Robotic Technology in the Workplace', Future of Work Hub, 04/12. https://www.futureofworkhub.info/comment/2019/12/4/robot-tax-the-pros-and-cons-of-taxing-robotic-technology-in-the-workplace
- Vincent, J., 2022. EU targets Big Tech with sweeping new antitrust legislation, *The Verge*, 24/03. https://www.theverge.com/2022/3/24/22994234/eu-antitrust-legislation-dma-digital-markets-act-details

—*In this field . . . only*: On algorithm regulation:

- Learned-Miller et al., 2020. *Facial Recognition Technologies in the Wild*, Algorithmic Justice League. https://www.ajl.org/federal-office-call

—*So gender . . . outside*: On organisational change from a feminist perspective:

- Acker, J., 2006. 'Inequality Regimes: Gender, Class, and Race in Organizations. *Gender & Society*, 20(4) 441–64. doi:10.1177/0891243206289499
- Walby, S., 2005. 'Introduction: Comparative gender

mainstreaming in a global era', *International Feminist Journal of Politics*, 7(4) 453–70. doi: 10.1080/14616740500284383

—*The first . . . people*: To know more about the ideas discussed in point 5:

- Cortina, L.M. and Areguin, M.A., 2021. 'Putting People Down and Pushing Them Out: Sexual Harassment in the Workplace', *Annual Review of Organizational Psychology and Organizational Behavior*, 8(1) 285–309.
- UNICEF, 2022. Gender and Innovation, Evidence briefs – insights into the gender digital divide for girls; What we know about the gender digital divide for girls: A literature review. https://www.unicef.org/eap/media/8311/file/What%20 we%20know%20about%20the%20gender%20digital%20 divide%20for%20girls:%20A%20literature%20review.pdf

—*For example, some of these ideas . . . medical assistance*: On the propositions I mention:

- Foxglove, 2020. 'Open letter from content moderators re: pandemic', 18/11. https://www.foxglove.org. uk/2020/11/18/open-letter-from-content-moderators-re-pandemic
- Houses of the Oireachtas (Irish National Parliament), Joint Committee on Enterprise, Trade and Employment debate, 2021. 'Online content moderation: discussion', 12/05. https://www.oireachtas.ie/en/debates/ debate/joint_committee_on_enterprise_trade_and_ employment/2021-05-12/2
- Royal Society for Arts, Manufactures and Commerce, 2017. Good Gigs, 26/04. https://www.thersa.org/reports/good-gigs-a-fairer-future-for-the-uks-gig-economy

—*Support new unions . . . efforts*: On workers' struggles in the tech sector:

- Tech Workers Coalition, 2020. 'A Tech Workers' Bill of Rights'. https://techworkerscoalition.org/bill-of-rights
- Coworker, 2022. 'Our Projects'. https://home.coworker.org/our-projects
- Jewell, H., 2022. *We Need Snowflakes! In defence of the sensitive, the angry and the offended.* Hachette.

—*Demand clearer . . . shopping choices*: On ethical consumption:

- Jones, E., 2019. 'Rethinking Greenwashing: Corporate Discourse, Unethical Practice, and the Unmet Potential of Ethical Consumerism', *Sociological Perspectives*, 62(5) 728–54. doi: 10.1177/0731121419849095

Conclusions

—*I will mention . . . us*: Some useful texts on the 'concrete' utopias I mention are:

- Bria, F. and Morozov, E., 2018. *Rethinking the Smart City. Democratizing Urban Technology*, Rosa Luxembourg Foundation, 22/01. https://rosalux.nyc/rethinking-the-smart-city
- Federici, S., 2018. *Re-enchanting the World: Feminism and the Politics of the Commons*, PM Press.
- Hernández Castillo, R.A., 2010. 'The Emergence of Indigenous Feminism in Latin America', *Signs: Journal of Women in Culture and Society*, 35(3), 539–45. doi: 10.1086/648538
- Mathiesen, K., 2012. 'The Human Right to Internet Access: A Philosophical Defense', *The International Review of Information Ethics*, 18(Dec), 9–22. doi: 10.29173/irie299

REFERENCES

- Parker, M., 2003. *Utopia and Organization*, Wiley-Blackwell.
- Yamamori, T., 2022. 'The Forgotten Feminist History of the Universal Basic Income', *History Workshop*, 04/04. https://www.historyworkshop.org.uk/the-forgotten-feminist-history-of-the-universal-basic-income

ACKNOWLEDGEMENTS

And lessons learned along the way

This is my first book, and as I wrote it I learned several far-from-banal things.

The first, which is very personal, is that the writing forms I normally engage in (academic papers, policy reports) give me a certain degree of protection from the subjects I am writing about. Let me explain myself further. For someone like me, who works daily on matters of gender-based violence, injustice and exploitation, it is not always easy to maintain the emotional detachment that is necessary to keep on doing the job. But, paradoxically, my having to comply with academic conventions and stylistic requirements has often offered me a protective filter and a defence mechanism. Working on this book, I have instead experimented with a different kind of writing, a way more subjective style. Many of those filters and defences have been pulled to pieces, and it hasn't always been easy. This is why I am immensely grateful to all those who, in different ways, accompanied, guided and supported me throughout this process, helping me find a new voice that suited my new goal.

Among these mentors and guides, I'd like to mention first of all my wonderful editors Hannah MacDonald and Charlotte Cole (September Publishing) and Marianna Aquino (Longanesi), and my agents Charlie Viney and Sam Edenborough, thanks to whom you are holding this book in your hands today. More generally, the September, Longanesi, Viney Agency and ILA teams have since day one believed in this book and have allowed it to come to fruition.

Apart from this professional support, while the book was in gestation I have also immensely benefitted from the input of the many extraordinary women (and yes, a few men too!) who I am lucky enough to have in my life. In particular, my writer friends Hannah Jewell, Zoë Guy-Sprague, Giorgia Tolfo and Roberta Zuric have generously provided feedback on early drafts and on the writing process. Equally generously, my novelist friend Marco Magini has offered advice based on his writing experience and his knowledge of the publishing world. My sister Ilaria Giugni and my cousin Barbara Celentani encouraged me at moments where writing felt hard, and have given me invaluable suggestions on several chapters. Belinda Bell, colleague, friend and role model, gifted me some of the most honest, sharp and useful counsel I got during the entire journey. And, more than anyone, my friend Francesca Di Nuzzo (the very same Francesca I talk about in Chapter 3) has spent several weekends reading different versions of the manuscript, sending me professional-level comments and discussing with me the possible trajectories of the text. Apart from being one of the people I cherish the most, Francesca has also shared with me many feminist struggles and I am grateful to the benign divinity (surely a goddess!) who made us meet back in 2010.

A second lesson I learned working on this book was that even when you are used to work on many things at once, at some point an endeavour as huge as writing your first book consumes you and invades every aspect of your daily life. This is why all my gratitude goes to my colleagues from the Cambridge Centre for Social Innovation and the OTIS group at the Cambridge Judge Business School at the University of Cambridge, and especially to CCSI directors Paul Tracey and Neil Stott, who offered me both the physical and mental space to work on this project, valuing and supporting me in every way. Those who work in my industry know that none of this should be taken for granted, and I'd like Paul and Neil to know that I never have.

On the other hand, without my extended family (my parents, my aunties, my cousins) and without the friends I have around me I would never have been able to set some boundaries and take care of myself as I wrote. My auntie Monetta Castiglione Morelli and my therapist Joan Kelly have been full of words of wisdom, and Elisabetta Brighi, Elena Cianci-Venturi, Emilia Del Franco, Federica Favuzza, Jole Fontana, Stefania Giannattasio, Laura Gutierrez-Gomez, Gabriella Iacobellis, Giulia Lasagni, Marzia Maccaferri, Marie Metzger, Marta Musso, Ryan Rafaty, Roberto Ricciardi, Stefano Santoro, Eleonora Sconci, Lera Shumaylova and, more than anyone else, my sweet yet indomitable sister Ilaria have reminded me, in their own different ways, that life is beautiful and filled with love, even when the combination of writing and lockdown started to feel a little heavy. I am blessed to know them all.

A third thing I already knew before starting this project but which

ACKNOWLEDGEMENTS

I understood way more profoundly afterwards is that putting a book together is neither an individual nor a solitary process. As many have observed before me, when writing one is always confronted with what has once been said, and with what is happening in the present. And indeed, in this volume, there are many voices alongside mine. To begin with, there are those of the women I interviewed. I cannot name them all, due to confidentiality reasons, yet I cannot help but mention Seyi Akiwowo, Jess Asato, Maria Bada, Lucy Delap, Alice Hutchings, Cathy Newman, Jess Phillips, Julie Ward, and my friends and fellow feminists Klementyna Suchanow and Viola Lo Moro.

Other voices I have constantly heard outside and inside me during the writing process have been those of the women whose words and deeds inspired me throughout the years, and of all the sister (and non-binary sibling) activists I met along the way. This time, too, I cannot mention everyone, but I'd like to cite at least the fabulous Silvana Agatone, Giorgia Carofiglio, Federica and Monica Cartelletti, Germana Cecconi, Thandeka Cochrane, Alessandra De Luca, Laura De Santis, Sara Di Rado, Ellen Davis-Walker, Irene Donadio, Venera Dimulescu, Carmen Ferrara, Serena Fiorletta, Nathalie Greenfield, Daniela Guercio, Serena Mammani, Alasia Nuti, Cristina Obber, Dolly Ogunrinde, Carla Panico, Samanta Picciaiola, Chiara Piccoli, Simone Phipps, Mariana Plaza, Francesca R. Recchia Luciani, Stella Rhode, Elyssa Rider, Luisa Rizzitelli, Lily Rosengard, Maria Grazia Sangalli, Margherita Santicchia, Jessica Sciarné, Clara Stella, Ciara Taylor, Ilaria Todde, Emrys Travis, Carolina Vesce, Vanessa Vizziello, Ottavia Voza, Emmanuela Wroth and Anna Zilli. Together with my partner in crime since 1987: my ally and indispensable friend Chiara De Santis. And to the many researchers and advocates involved in our think tank GenPol, which Chiara, Francesca, Ellen and I co-founded a few years ago.

This book, as you might have noticed, includes some suggestions situated at the intersection between gender, social and ecological justice. For this reason, much of the energy I have exchanged throughout the years with a bunch of very smart comrades-in-arms has also ended up in it. Among them there are: Francesco Bilotta, Yàdad de Guerre, Tiziano Distefano, Tobias Müller, Mauro Pinto, Luca Recano, Antonio Rotelli and Tanner Taddeo. My marvellous students, who regularly inspire me to ask myself better questions and look for better answers, have also been a great source of inspiration. Some of them specifically stimulated me to reflect on matters of gender, economic and digital justice, and they include: Sarah Awan, Eunice Baguma Ball, Wernhard Berger, Ann Carroll, Mary Galeti, Nasreen Khan, Caitlyn Merry, Rebecca Moe, Joellen Nicholson, Anna Maria Raul Casas, Jessica Rose, Chen-Ta Sung and Seira Yun. I also want to thank my colleagues Stephanie Creary, Tom Lawrence, Nelson Phillips and, again, my wonderful mentor Paul Tracey for having pushed me to think differently about oppression and resistance. All of them inspired me in multiple ways, but I am the only one responsible for any mistakes in this text.

I would also like to thank all of the organisations who allowed me to start presenting in writing or in-person findings connected with this book, which often ended up generating new viewpoints. Among these, social enterprises Beyond Equality and SOS Music Media, research and practitioner network CODE, FEPS (and particularly Laeticia Thissen), Antinoo Arcigay Napoli, the Cambridge Festival of Ideas (thanks to the amazing, caring Pam Mungroo), the Cambridge Judge Business School, European Women's Lobby,

IPPF European Network, GayNews, Italy's Rete Nazionale per il Contrasto ai Discorsi e ai Fenomeni d'Odio (thanks to Paola Rizzi), Giulia Giornaliste, Aidos, the University of Trento, Falling Book, Zona Franca, Fondazione Feltrinelli, *Globe Post*, *Che Fare* and, yet again, GenPol, thanks above all to the work of Chiara De Santis and Ellen Davis-Walker.

Finally, there is one last truth that while writing I have felt even more viscerally and profoundly than usual. Writing a book is not simply a labour of love, but also an enormous privilege, especially for a woman or any person deprived, through history, of the right to speak and tell one's story. Plus, as famously summarised by Virginia Woolf in her celebrated essay *A Room of One's Own*, many women do not end up becoming authors because they lack the means: from the economic and material stability essential to sit down and write, to the emotional and intellectual freedom stemming from having 'a room of one's own'.

Thanks to my mum and dad, Maria Rosaria Castiglione Morelli and Maurizio Giugni, I had everything I needed. To them both (as well as to Nella Castiglione Morelli, to Stefano Chiappetta and to Gigliola Rocco, to whom this work is dedicated) I also owe a certainty which was instilled in me as a child: if I have something to say, someone will be there to listen. And that really is no small thing. By putting this into writing I am not trying to disclaim or diminish my personal achievements, of which I remain proud, but I am trying to put them into context and to remember that they are not only mine.

Last but not least, it must be said that during a time as complex as a global pandemic I was able to devote time and energy to thinking and writing thanks to my life partner Adam Fellows. Every day, back home after hours of experiments in his university lab, Adam cooked me dinner, made tea at 2 a.m. and coffee in the early morning, and he reminded me when I needed a break. Among the millions of other ways in which he has been supporting me, Adam has also read various versions of the manuscript, helped me make sense of my Post-it notes when I hardly understood them myself and listened for hours to the accounts of injustice I sought to depict in the book, marching alongside me to ask for solutions whenever he has been able to. Adam does not need to read the feminist treaties on the concept of care I suggest in the References, for I have seen him putting that very concept into practice from the earliest times of our relationship. I'm a lucky woman.

© Alex Saunderson

Dr Lilia Giugni is a feminist activist, a lecturer in Social Innovation at the University of Bristol and a researcher at the Cambridge Centre for Social Innovation at the University of Cambridge. She co-founded the think tank GenPol – Gender & Policy Insights, holds a PhD in Politics from the University of Cambridge and is a Fellow of the Royal Society of Arts. Her research interests and advocacy work focus on violence against women and girls, the gendered side of technology and innovation, and the intersections between gender, racial and social injustice. A multidisciplinary researcher, she sits on the board of several charities, social enterprises and feminist networks. She regularly writes articles on women's rights and delivers talks and keynote speeches internationally.

T: @liliagiugni